BY THE LINN ROCKS

The Story of East Linton and the Parish of Prestonkirk

Foreword by The Rt. Hon. the Lord Briggs, FBA

EAST LINTON LOCAL HISTORY SOCIETY

This book is dedicated to the men of East Linton and the Parish of Prestonkirk who laid down their lives in two World Wars.

First published 1999
Reprinted 2003
Published by the East Linton Local History Society 1999
Printed in Scotland by D & J Croal Limited, Haddington

David K. Affleck
Derek G. H. Andrews
Michael Beilby
Monica Cameron
Douglas Cullen
Rosamond Cullen
Liz Denley
John W. Denning
Earle M. S. Douglas
Penny Durman
Roger Durman
Drew Easton
Jim Fraser
Dennis Garvie
Iain F. Govan
John G. Guy
Robert Halpin
Margaret Hamilton
Mrs E. Hannah
Marion Herkes
Bill Jeffrey
Elizabeth Jeffrey
Douglas B. Law
Rosemary Lincoln
Ken Lochhead
Jean McKinnon
Tom Middlemass
Garry S. Menzies
Jim Menzies
Margaret E. Morrison
Bill Patterson
David S. Ritchie
John W. Steele
'Steve' Stevenson
Jane Stevenson
Romaine Strang
Nan Sutherland
Chris Tabraham
Gordon Tait
Mrs A. Thomson
Donald Watson

ISBN 0 9535974 0 7

CONTENTS

ILLUSTRATIONS

COLOUR PLATES

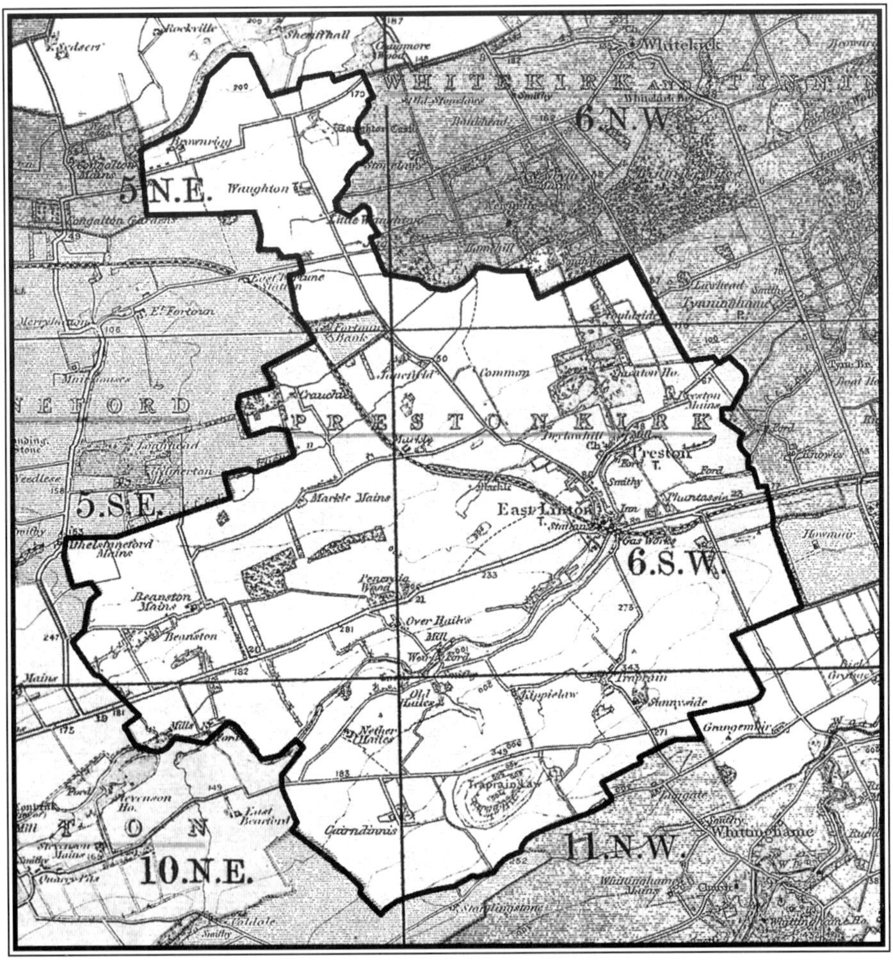

[1] Prestonkirk Parish c.1900

FOREWORD

by

The Rt. Hon. The Lord Briggs, F. B. A.

Local history is one of the most vigorous branches of the subject, and local history societies - for various reasons - now thrive in many parts of the world, not least in East Lothian. The flourishing East Linton Local History Society has produced this informative and interesting story of East Linton and the Parish of Prestonkirk which is an excellent example of individual and collective research in action. The authors are too modest to tell the story of their own Society as part of their bigger story. Indeed, they devote only a brief chapter of their book to the twentieth century. I hope they will turn their attention next to the last 50 years of local history when oral and visual history for the first time provide a new basis for local as well as for national and international studies of the past.

I was honoured and delighted to be asked by David Ritchie to write this foreword. I have always been interested in local history, beginning to write about it before it had reached its boom period in the 1960s; and I have a special personal interest in *By the Linn Rocks* since for the last eight years I have been living in Tyninghame and shopping (and much else) in East Linton. Every detail of the story told in this book means far more to me now than it would have done 10 years ago, and some of the details, which I did not know, already make me look at places and things, people and institutions, events and processes in a different way.

I have always believed that local history is interesting and important for two reasons. First, in its own right, it enables us to travel through time and recover lost experience in a place which is close to us. We contrast, but we also recognise the experience of our ancestors. Some of our individual and family experience is new, some repeat the experience of others long ago. We appreciate this relationship most clearly through local history. Second, local history provides the foundation for a richer version of national and international history, whether it be the history of Scotland or of

England, of Europe or, spanning the oceans, as so many Scots did, of the world. Until recently local history was used largely to illustrate accepted versions of national, continental or world history through the examples that it provided. Now we are starting to build upwards from it and produce new versions on firmer foundations.

Local histories are best, I believe, when they span centuries, as this history does. Historians should never say 'that is not my period', however much they may look to other specialist historians for advice: they should be time travellers, and because time is related to place, the study of topography becomes both a historical and a geographical enquiry.

The importance of place comes out very clearly in the pages that follow, explicitly in the chapter on parish place names, and implicitly throughout every chapter. The authors do what they must do - that is, make their readers want to explore particular places for themselves. I now understand far more about Phantassie - and the name has not lost its romance in the process - and Traprain than I ever did, and I now have a completely new mental map of East Lothian and of the Parish of Prestonkirk. Even before the book is published I will now start looking at familiar sites and sights in a new way. I know, however, that I now need both a physical and social map as companions to the book.

The return to the beginnings of history in Chapter 1 is particularly fascinating. Getting to know our remote ancestors - and many crucial details concerning them will never be known - is no substitute for getting to know even more - as we can - about our recent ancestors. We can find out more and more about them. Yet remote history immediately takes us back through history into geography and geology and meteorology. Once we are in 'medieval times' we are already in more familiar territory. I have felt that in other parts of Scotland, particularly Orkney.

The three modern centuries, given separate chapters in this book, are inevitably treated very selectively, but the authors place religion where it ought to be placed and deal with economic and social change as neatly as they can. Change, however initiated - and individuals took the lead in the process - transformed both the environment and the people who lived in it in ways that their ancestors could not foresee and which they themselves did not fully comprehend. Demography is often at the base here, family history always. The labels which we attach to social structures and to historical processes, like 'feudalism', 'industrialisation', 'urbanisation', 'secularisation', are never adequate, however useful, even necessary, though they may be. We can scarcely write about what King David I did or about what Adam Smith wrote without using them.

Two points in the story told by East Linton Local History Society linger in my mind - first, the significance of communications - with the Linton bridge over the Tyne (Linton-Briggis, a name that appeals to me), built in the sixteenth century as a symbol - and, second, the conclusion to the first paragraph in the last chapter which introduces a section called 'conservation and change'.

The fortunes of the bridge at East Linton can be dealt with more quickly by historians than they could be by successive past generations of local inhabitants who were forced to keep the bridge in order after 1549 when the French tried to demolish it during the siege of Haddington. It was not demolished, but for 200 years there was an argument about who should pay for repairs and upkeep. In 1666 the Privy Council (no less) acknowledged at the same time its importance in communications between Scotland and England and its ruinous state.

The last chapter, following notable chapters on local clubs, artists and societies, suggests that however many changes have taken place in the twentieth century - and they have been far-reaching and pervasive - 'the long association [of East Linton] with so many artists and their work has developed in the people an appreciation of the place and some caution about removing the features in the interests of so-called progress'. It was surely not only artists, well described one-by-one, who have reinforced the strong local sense that while there is usually a need for adaptation there is always a need for conservation. No one in East Linton or East Lothian should ever assume without question that change means progress.

The Linton bridge is not the only bridge to figure in *By the Linn Rocks.* We read too of John Rennie's bridges - not only of his famous Waterloo Bridge in London, but of the nearby bridge at Musselburgh which, when opened in 1806, led the Provost to declare that it was 'nae brig at a'. Ye dinnae ken when you're on it or aff it'. Rennie was an engineer who moved from mechanical to civil engineering, a change of status as well as of occupation, and he is one of the many people in these pages who merit and sometimes have inspired detailed biographies.

The 'fact boxes' in this book sometimes cover biographies, brief lives of the kind which Samuel Smiles in nearby Haddington liked to tell. It will be interesting if, as I hope, a sequel appears, to see what topics are picked out for 'the fact boxes' of the late - twentieth and twenty-first centuries. Nonetheless, this book, which I have read with great attention has an endearing quality which goes beyond facts. There is enthusiasm too - and commitment. Many of the sentences - a higher proportion than in most books - end with an exclamation mark. These demonstrate that a discovery has been made by the author which he or she feels merits personal response and demands a collective response which he or she is sure will be forthcoming. There are fewer question marks in the text, but there will be more of these as readers respond. One question answered provokes another. Meanwhile, history goes on even when a millennium - and not just a century - ends; a committee of different groups in East Linton has been set up to decide how to celebrate it. This book appears at a particularly appropriate time. A seal is fixed on our present as well as on our recorded past.

Asa Briggs

Tyninghame, March 1999

INTRODUCTION

The parish of Prestonkirk, East Lothian, with its town of East Linton, possesses many features which have given it a long, rich and distinguished place in Scottish history. The parish is divided by the River Tyne running from the west to the North Sea in a north-easterly direction. The historic main route south from Scotland down the east coast of England, known as the Great North Road, had to cross the river at some point. Until 1928, this crossing was made by a sixteenth-century stone bridge over the rocky linn, or water cascade, at East Linton.

The fall of the River Tyne at the linn provided the power to drive several mills around which clustered a community serving the surrounding agricultural area. The bridge assumed an additional strategic importance in time of war when invading armies marched and counter-marched along the main route to and from the English Border.

The low-lying fertile soils of the parish together with the higher ground to the south, especially Traprain Law, made the area attractive to early farmers, with an escape to the hills in time of danger. Lying in the lea of the hills to the south and west, the parish enjoys some of the best sunshine in the country with adequate rainfall, earning it the title of the 'market garden of Scotland'. With these advantages it is perhaps not surprising that it was the lairds and farmers from this area who took the opportunity, after the cessation of centuries of hostilities, to come to the forefront of the agricultural revolution in the late eighteenth century.

Nor is it surprising that towards the end of the nineteenth century artists flocked to the parish, to capture on canvas its special quality of light, its attractive landscape of fields, tree-lined river and warm-coloured stone buildings with their red pantile roofs.

It is against this background that the East Linton Local History Society has endeavoured, within the confines of these pages, to tell the story, from national and local records, of the lives and personalities who have lived in the parish, from the earliest times to the present day.

By the twelfth century AD, Lothian was fully within the Kingdom of Scotland and organised into parishes. If the parish bounds have remained reasonably constant down the years, the name certainly has not. In 1127 there is a reference to Lintoun ('the settlement by the torrent'), and in 1342 to the nearby church of 'Hauche' (or 'Haugh'), which describes its situation close by a riverside meadow. The establishment of a house of Red Friars close by the church led to the name of Preston ('priests' settlement') and to Prestonhaugh. As such it was known until the early eighteenth century when the present name of Prestonkirk came into general use. To distinguish the parish from the church we have called them 'Prestonkirk' and 'Preston Kirk' respectively.

Grateful thanks are due to all those in the East Linton Local History Society who have contributed parts of the story and to its compilation.

On behalf of the Society, I would also wish to acknowledge the following for their valued contributions:

Janice Tabraham for book layout and design;
David Henrie for colour photography;
Roy Stewart Print Services for print management.

Finally, the Society gratefully acknowledges the generous financial assistance given by 'Awards for All' and the Friends of Prestonkirk Parish Church.

David S. Ritchie

Chapter 1

REMOTE ANCESTORS

Prehistoric farmers

For several millennia after the last major glaciers melted in Scotland the level of the sea varied above and below the present level. At times animals and people were able to migrate westward across what is now the North Sea from the continent to Britain. About 4000 BC the sea would have been much higher, so that the linn (from the Old English *hlynn*, 'torrent') at East Linton would have been about the tidal limit. Tyninghame, Knowes, Binning Wood and up the Peffer Burn to Markle Mains would have been mud flats or shallow water, leaving Drylaw Hill, Smeaton and Lawhead as a promontory flanked by tidal sea.

Humans have been in our area for about 8000 years, but it was only from about 4000 BC that these early hunter-gatherers began to put down roots. They cleared the forests both to create pastures for growing crops and herding domestic animals for meat and milk, but also to provide greater safety from bears and wolves. Once farming was established these Neolithic people would have found the area around the Tyne estuary ideal, with the well-drained gravel soils suitable for cultivation.

These first farmers have generally left few traces behind in southern Scotland, much of the evidence having probably been destroyed by cultivation. Until recently the only sign of their presence in the vicinity of East Linton was a few artefacts - pottery, polished stone axes and arrowheads found at places like Hedderwick Hill and in the manse garden at Whittingehame. That is until an important Neolithic complex was discovered by aerial photography in 1981 in the field between Preston Kirk and Drylawhill to the north.

Royal Commission on the Ancient and Historical Monuments of Scotland

[2] The Neolithic complex showing up as crop-marks in the field between Preston Kirk (bottom left) and Drylawhill.

The crop-marks were identified as the remains of a cursus, or ceremonial enclosure, and rectilinear settlements. The long, narrow cursus is 60m wide and in excess of 300m long (the parallel ditches, orientated east-west, disappear under the drive-way to Smeaton). It is one of only 30 or so recorded in Scotland, and although it remains unexcavated, and thus undated, evidence from elsewhere suggests that these places of prehistoric power date from about 3300 BC.

From about 2000 BC major changes are found in the archaeological record. These include the practice of burying an individual in a stone-lined grave, called a cist, more often than not accompanied by a finely made pot known as a Beaker. Several of these box-like tombs have been found in and around the parish, including on the summit of Traprain Law, at Phantassie in 1927 and most recently (1992) in a field at Preston Mains. Sometimes the long, flat stones forming the cist were decorated with cup-and-ring markings; the large cap-stone covered with such marks found in 1996 beside a field between East Linton and Markle, and now in the Museum of Scotland, was most probably originally from a nearby cist burial.

Such cist burials were probably of important people, and it is possible that the three standing stones in the parish (there are only six in the entire county) also mark the graves of local chiefs. One standing stone, known locally as the 'Long Stane', stands prominently beside the A1 on the eastern slope of Pencraig. The other two stones once stood close beside each other on Cairndinnis Farm to the west of Traprain Law; one was removed to Standingstone Farm, just inside Morham parish, in the nineteenth century; the remaining one, the so-called Loth Stone, takes its name from the legendary figure whom King Arthur made king of Lothian.

The most profound change that occurred, however, was the introduction of bronze working, for making items such as axes, swords and horse harness. Evidence for bronze-working has come from archaeological excavations on Traprain Law, which produced moulds for casting bronze axes. But such metals were rare and probably used mainly by privileged groups; it was not a technological Bronze Age for the ordinary farming household in the parish in the second millennium BC.

The spread of technology using iron, which appeared around 700 BC, caused even greater political and cultural changes. The metal resources for bronze had been scarce and localised, whereas iron ores were much more widely available, so that the supply of tools and weapons could not be so readily retained in the hands of the few.

Archaeologists have changed the former picture of life in this area in the late centuries BC from that of a sparse population of primitive tribesmen to one of densely settled areas with small farms raising grain crops and livestock. There is evidence that Celtic speech was in use by 600 BC and possibly earlier. There would have been a firmly stratified social structure with a privileged aristocracy, and the majority of the population in relative or absolute servility.

Chris Tabraham

[3] The prehistoric standing stone (the 'Long Stane') on Pencraig with the ridged hump of Traprain Law in the distance.

In the shadow of Rome

By the first century AD the inhabitants of this area were using a language very close to the ancestor of modern Welsh. Their aristocratic and learned classes, at least, would have been able to converse with any similarly ranking natives of Britain to the south of them, and probably also with those north of the Tay. The name by which the Romans distingished the people of Lothian from neighbouring groups was *Votadini.* This tribe was consistently friendly to the Romans, who extended their influence into northern Britain in the late first century, defeating a Caledonian army at Mons Graupius, in Aberdeenshire, in 79. But it appears that the Votadini offered no resistance for there are no traces of military works or conflicts in their area.

Meanwhile undefended rural settlements flourished in Lothian. More than a dozen are known in the vicinity of Traprain alone. Since the Votadini were a relatively small tribe next to the most powerful tribal confederation in Britain, the Brigantes of northern England, under the realpolitik principle that 'my enemy's enemy is my friend', it is not surprising that the Votadini allied themselves with Rome. Similarly they may have been glad to see a source of trouble from north of the Forth dealt with. Moreover, those who controlled the area's agricultural wealth must have had an enviable business opportunity to supply the thousands of Roman soldiers and numerous officials stationed at Inveresk and Cramond. It does seem to be the case that the Votadini used their alliance with Rome to protect their stable and successful economy, as well as ward off potentially aggressive neighbours.

By the end of the third century the Romans were referring to the northern tribes as *Picti* ('painted ones'), which may suggest some confederation of which the Votadini were not a part. By the early fourth century Pictish raiding was requiring punitive action by Roman emperors. The generations of Roman influence south of the Forth must have alienated the Votadini from the Picts in language, social customs and attitudes, particularly when Christianity started to spread among the Romanised tribes.

We can imagine lookouts stationed at times of threat on places like Traprain Law, watching for the boats of raiding parties descending from the north. By 360 the Gaelic-speaking *Scoti* were coming across from Ireland to join the Picts in ravaging places near the frontier. At the same time German groups from across the North Sea were attacking southern Britain.

It was in these last years before the final withdrawal of Roman forces from Britain in 410 that the Traprain Law Treasure, a great hoard of cut-up Roman silverware, was deposited. It has been suggested that the hoard was a pay-off by Imperial Rome to the Votadini for services rendered and expected, indicating that the relationship with Rome had ended much as it had begun.

The identity, language and Celtic Iron-Age ways of the Votadini had survived the centuries of Roman influence. After the Roman withdrawal, the tribal name, Votadini, lost its plural ending in 'i' and evolved with the native British language into 'Gododdin'.

Traprain Law

Traprain Law, with its steep sides and flat top arising out of fertile lowland, is without doubt the single most important prehistoric monument in the parish - indeed in all East Lothian. From its summit has come evidence of its use as a Bronze-Age burial place around 1500 BC (the denuded remains of a stone burial cairn can be seen to the east of the Ordnance Survey trig point), and from 1000 BC onwards as a thriving fortified settlement. This continued through the Iron Age, into and beyond the Roman era.

Excavations earlier this century shed new light on this puzzling ancient site. Layer upon layer of fragmentary stone and timber houses were found surviving under the turf, testimony to the long occupation of the Law. These houses are scarcely visible today, with the exception of the stone foundations of a large circular building near the trig point on the summit which has in the past been thought of as a sheepfold but which seems more likely to have been an important prehistoric building.

The houses may no longer be visible, but the defences are still very much in evidence, particularly along the west and north sides. These stone ramparts, with their impressively wide entrances, show signs of having been rebuilt several times. The area enclosed by these defences is roughly equivalent to the medieval centre of the nearby market town of Haddington, and there has been a tendency to view the Law like a modern town. But the evidence suggests that the Law may not always have functioned as a permanent settlement. It may also have been used as a major meeting-place, where folk met to celebrate festivals. The permanent homes of the prehistoric farmers were more likely situated on the lower-lying ground round about the Law, such as inside the far smaller hillfort above the Orchard on the eastern slope of Pencraig, and in circular enclosures like that beside Houston Mill. Both of these sites were recently discovered by aerial photography.

Undoubtedly the most startling discovery made on the Law came in 1919 when the famous Treasure was found. Dating from the reign of Emperor Honorius (395-423), it comprised silver bowls, spoons, flagons, dishes and plates of Roman origin. All the pieces had been cut up and flattened, perhaps in preparation for melting down, before being deliberately buried. It is not clear how the Votadini got their hands on this material or what they intended to use it for. Was it a diplomatic gift from the Empire perhaps? Could it have been obtained through trading links? Or was it simply loot from raids made into Roman territory to the south? We shall never know.

Historic Scotland

[4] Traprain Law looking south towards the Lammermuir Hills.

National Museums of Scotland

[5] Horse and chariot trappings found on Traprain Law.

The eclipse of the Gododdin

After the Roman withdrawal, the remainder of the first millennium AD has been described as the 'Dark Ages'. There were major and sometimes violent movements of people into Britain from Germany and Ireland in the earlier centuries, and important settlements from Norway and Denmark in the later centuries.

By the late sixth century the Gododdin were certainly Christian and under pressure from the heathen Angles, settled in the southern parts of the old Votadini territory, now Northumberland. The epic British poem, *y Gododdin*, composed about 600 at Din Eidyn (Edinburgh Castle rock), the court of the Gododdin king, Mynyddog Mwynfawr 'the wealthy', by Aneirin his bard, describes the gallant but doomed attempt of the 'Men of the North' to repel the heathen invaders. All but a handful of Mynyddog's 300-strong warband fell in battle at Catraeth (Catterick) in North Yorkshire.

In 603 the Scots, by now strongly established in Argyllshire as the kingdom of Dal Riata, contested unsuccessfully with the Angles at the battle of Degsastan (possibly Dawston in Liddesdale) for control of the crumbling tribal kingdoms of southern Scotland. Thereafter there was little to stop the advance of Anglian control up the coast into Lothian. Place-names such as Tyninghame (*Tiningaham*, 'village of those dwelling by the River Tyne'), and Whittingehame (*Hwitingaham*, 'settlement of Hwita's people') indicate some Anglian settlement under way from as early as the second quarter of the seventh century. The field name Laringham Hill, east of the road to Stenton, may be another of this early group, recorded as *Lyneryngham* in the late middle ages.

Until King Oswald (634-41) called in missionaries from Iona, the Northumberland élite still worshipped Germanic gods. Nevertheless, there can be no doubt that a new language, the Northumbrian dialect of Anglo-Saxon, was now to be increasingly heard in the lower Tyne valley and in the shadow of Traprain Law.

St. Kentigern, who was more affectionately known as Mungo, was a real person who evangelised Strathclyde from a base in Glasgow and died about 614. However, the stories about the origins of Kentigern and his mother Taneu (or Thenew; she was also known as Enoch), the daughter of King Loth of Traprain Law, belong to legend, more informative about the people who preserved and recorded them and their motives than about dim and distant events. It is impossible that St. Kentigern could have, as in one story, granted churches to St. Baldred (or Bealdhere) of Tyninghame, for the latter died in 756. However, the place-name Preston, which has given its name to our parish, is Old English and indicates that a church was founded before or during Baldred's time. Kentigern is remembered by his nick-name at Mungoswells near Aberlady. His local associations lived in memory into the sixteenth century or were revived by those with antiquarian knowledge, as in the name Kentigern Hepburn of Waughton, a member of the local aristocracy who fell at Flodden in 1513.

Since Tyninghame, where Baldred founded his monastery, belonged to the monks of Lindisfarne, it is likely that it was at the latter that Baldred had been trained. His name is Old English, though this does not mean that he could not have had Gododdin ancestry. Baldred is described as taking a great interest in the local traditions about Kentigern, and some of the surviving stories about Kentigern are full of geographical details of the area between East Linton and Aberlady. That topographical detail could have been part of the stories taken to Strathclyde by refugees from the collapse of Gododdin power within a generation after Kentigern's death.

Thus the associations of Kentigern with the royal family of the Gododdin and its capital on Traprain Law owe much to folk traditions of a once-great status for the hill, and to Celtic folk tales about miraculous escapes. Nevertheless it is not beyond possibility that Glasgow's patron saint had his origin among the native élite in this area.

St. Baldred

St. Baldred was a holy man about whom little of fact is known but whose undoubted piety made such a profound impression on the folk of this part of East Lothian that he continues to be revered to this day.

Some hold to a late medieval tradition, printed in the *Aberdeen Breviary* of 1510, that he was a contemporary of St Kentigern, Bishop of Glasgow, and that he lived the life of a hermit on the Bass Rock until his death in 608. Others follow Symeon of Durham who, writing in the early twelfth century, recorded that '...the man of the Lord and priest Baldred, who had led in Tyninghame the life of an anchorite, trod the way of the holy fathers, departing on 6 March in the 20th year of the reign of King Egbert of Northumbria (ie, 756)'.

Whatever the truth of the matter, clearly Baldred was instrumental in nourishing a Christian tradition in this part of Lothian. Stories abound of his miraculous powers, stories that belong to the realm of myth rather than history. But the curious tale of how, on his death, his body miraculously became three bodies, thereby allowing all three of his congregations at Prestonkirk, Tyninghame and Auldhame to have him as their own, testifies to the reverence and admiration they all had for this simple man of God.

So grateful were they in fact that they named several natural features after him, like St. Baldred's Well and St. Baldred's Whirl, or pool, in the Tyne below Preston Kirk, and St. Baldred's Boat, Cave and Cradle along the coast. It is also recorded that a huge statue of him used to stand at Preston Kirk until 1770 when it was broken up at the time of the rebuilding of the main part of the church.

A Prayer for St. Baldred
(from the Aberdeen Breviary*)*
O God, who through the contemplative life of the blessed Baldred, thy bishop and confessor, hast conferred ineffable grace on thy servants; grant, we beseech thee, that by his merits and intercessions we may be able to obtain in all things the saving help of thy mercy.
Through our Lord. Amen.

Chris Tabraham

[6] The St Baldred window in Preston Kirk, designed by William Wilson and installed in 1959.

Picts and Vikings

By 685 Northumbrian influence and partial control had spread beyond the Forth into Pictland. However, in that year the Northumbrians, under King Ecgfrith, were decisively defeated by the Pictish king, Bridei, at Nechtansmere (Dunnichen), in Angus. Northumbria's heyday as the greatest of the English kingdoms was over and it never again tried to expand beyond the Forth.

The Picts ventured south of the Forth. Even so, Northumbria held on in the eighth century to its Lothian lands and managed to expand its control in the west from Galloway into Ayrshire. At times both Picts and Northumbrians weakened themselves with civil wars, oblivious to the threat that was looming from the north. Lothian would have been an insecure and vulnerable place.

In 793 came the first Viking raid on Lindisfarne, news of which struck terror into people far up and down the Northumbrian coast. These raids for several decades consisted of freelance plundering of easy targets such as rich monasteries, but by the later ninth century Danes were causing serious trouble in England with organised armies and a permanent presence aimed at conquest and settlement. In 867 Northumbria fell to Guthrum's Danish army, and there is ample evidence in recorded history, archaeology and place-names for a Viking kingdom based in York and for widespread Viking settlement in much of eastern England. However, the introduction of Viking names becomes sporadic north of the Wear and very rare north of the Tweed.

Meanwhile Kenneth macAlpin, who had united the kingdoms of the Picts and the Scots in about 843, was the first to make that arrangement permanent with a new dynasty in which succession was open to a smaller kin group than before. Under pressure from expanding Norse encroachments in the islands and western coastal fringes and Norse sea power, the Gaels of Alba were cut off from their Irish origins and had to look east and south for survival and expansion. Kenneth wrested Lothian from Northumbria and controlled the Pictish area with ruthless destruction of resistance. The Gaelic language replaced Pictish within a few generations and Scottish laws were imposed.

Lothian and the kingdom of Scotland

In 900 Constantin II became king of Alba, the new official name for the combined kingdom. Under his influence Strathclyde became more integrated with Gaelic-speaking Alba while he skilfully played off the rival Danish and Norse Viking factions against each other, changing alliances as necessary. However, the West Saxon King Athelstan who controlled much of England harried eastern Scotland in 934 and was victorious at Brunanburh (probably Burnswark in Dumfriesshire) three years later. Athelstan's death in 939 allowed the return to York of the Viking King Olaf Gothfrithsson, and two years later Olaf's men sacked St Baldred's monastery at Tyninghame.

After the death in battle in 954 of the Viking ruler of York, Eric Bloodaxe, Wessex gained temporary control of the whole of England, but was not strong enough to prevent the fall of Din Eidyn and Lothian to Constantin's son, Indulf. The annexation of Lothian from English control was recognised in about 973 by Edgar, king of a united England, and in 1018 Malcolm II, King of Scots (1005-1034), a direct descendant of Kenneth macAlpin, soundly defeated Earl Uhtred of Bernicia at Carham on the Tweed. In the ensuing treaty Scotland's eastern Border at the Tweed was regularised. From that time on Lothian has retained its Scottish identity.

Chapter 2

PARISH PLACE-NAMES

The origin of place-names

All the place-names in the parish, including those with elements ultimately from Latin or Greek, are wholly from languages within the Indo-European group which spread out from the steppes of eastern Europe to as far as Ireland and India. With the possible exception of the name *Tyne*, which may well have been here long before any Celtic tongue, all the remaining names belong to one of two main branches of the Celtic group, or to varieties of speech mainly descended from that of the Angles, Saxons and other tribes who settled in southern Britain from Germany and southern Scandinavia after the Romans left.

One of the less well known facts of the succession of languages in this area is that there was a presence of Gaelic speakers from the mid- to late-tenth century until at least the twelfth, so the Gaelic names are actually centuries younger than the oldest of the 'English' names. For some generations around 1000 years ago there may have been communities or households within quite short distances of each other speaking mutually incomprehensible languages, Old English (or Anglo-Saxon), Gaelic which had come in from north of the Forth after the Scottish conquest of Lothian, and a northern dialect of Welsh (also known as Brythonic or Cumbric). This last was descended from the language of the Votadini, a tongue close to the Celtic of the near continent, which had probably already been in the area for some generations BC. Although we know that Welsh and Gaelic are quite closely related, their speakers then are unlikely to have had any awareness of that, let alone of a common 'Celtic' identity; whereas educated speakers of Old English knew very well that their tongue was akin to that of their German cousins across the North Sea.

Celtic names

The parish's oldest local name, as is often the case, is the river name TYNE. It is typically very short and probably had a very simple descriptive meaning. There are similar names to Tyne in England and on the Continent. Its form may be Celtic or pre-Celtic and may just mean 'the flowing one'.

Chris Tabraham

[7] The River Tyne above the ford at Knowes Mill.

Ancient Celtic names are usually straightforward, no-nonsense descriptions of the geography or man-made features useful in an age before maps. The names may originate from well before Northumbrian rule was established in Lothian in the earlier seventh century, but some could be later, as the older language probably survived in pockets for generations or even several centuries. The fact that the English-speaking settlers did not wipe out the local population but mixed, or co-existed, with it is indicated by the retention of so many older names, and by the survival to this day of the Celtic stress pattern of names like *Pencraig* and *Traprain*.

CAIRNDINNIS appears in several variants in eighteenth-century maps. The second part should be from the Welsh *dinas*, a fortification, especially one used for emergency refuge rather than permanent occupation, as was probably the state of Traprain Law after Roman times. The first part is less certain. There is no obvious cairn for it to refer to. Just possibly it is from *cardden*, a copse or small wood, which happens to fit the geography of Cairndinnis Farm now: so 'copse of fort'. One of the eighteenth-century forms gives another possibility: 'crag of fort'

DUNPENDER, the older name of Traprain Law, is probably a corruption of *Din pelydr*, 'fort of (spear) shafts'. This very old name would refer to the appearance of the enclosure on Traprain Law at some stage, possibly centuries BC. The Celtic *dun/din* also appears in French names like Verdun and Autun and is related to Germanic words such as English *town*, German *zaun* (fence) and Dutch *tuin* (garden). The basic sense is 'enclosure', though *din* seems to have become confused with a similar Celtic word meaning 'hill'.

PEFFER is another ancient name given to watercourses. *Pefr* means 'radiant, shining, beautiful', which seems strange for a muddy agricultural drainage ditch. However, before drainage it was more of a broad marsh than a burn, and in wet periods must have gathered water from the surrounding land to become a shallow loch, shining once the sun came out. This characteristic of sometimes wide-spreading waters over a flood plain or basin was shared with other Peffers, including the Peffer of Peffermill in Edinburgh and those in Perthshire and Ross-shire (one of many indicators from place-names that Picts spoke a closely related language or dialect to the other Britons farther south). Similar names occur in south-west Britain. A more prosaic explanation of the 'radiance' would be that it referred not to waters sparkling in the sun but to the tendency of the waters to spread or 'radiate' far from their dry-weather limits.

PENCRAIG (earlier Pencraik or Pencraick) is also found in Herefordshire and there are many similar names in Wales. It appears to mean 'head or end (Welsh *pen*) of crag'; there is a small crag on the north side. However, a derivation from pen and crug ('head or end of ridge', or possibly 'head or chief ridge') would make more obvious sense of the topography. *Crug* is related to Scots *rigg*/ English *ridge*, and German *rücken*, meaning 'back'.

TRAPRAIN is of course Tra-prain, not Trap-rain, and is one of several Tra- names in southern Scotland, corresponding to the countless Tre- names of Wales and Cornwall. This element *tref* simply means a settlement or farmstead. The second part is probably from *pren*, 'tree'. The likely meaning is thus simply 'tree settlement'. It may imply that the landscape was already so cleared of native forest that any woods or large individual trees were notable features in the landscape, but may refer to a sacred tree or pole such as Celtic and Germanic peoples revered.

Old English names

Place-names deriving from Old English include most obviously LINTON. In England it generally refers to the growing of linen, but our Linton is more probably derived from the torrent (Old English *hlynn*) crossed by the ancient bridge.

MARKLE has had many odd forms over the centuries, but from the early forms such as Nethirmerkhill it probably represents *mearc hyll*, 'boundary hill', from the ridge of Pencraig. There is no parish boundary there, so the reference may be to some long-lost estate boundary. It certainly has nothing to do with the 'miracle' of the legendary Battle of Athelstaneford. Marcle in Herefordshire has a slightly different origin, as 'boundary clearing' or 'boundary wood'.

PRESTON is a very common term in England, from *preost-tun*, 'priest's settlement', or *preosta-tun*, 'priests' settlement'. Our Preston refers to the ancient church site associated with St. Baldred. PRESTONKIRK is a relatively recent formation. Old English *preost* came through church Latin from Greek *presbyteros*, 'elder/older', so that both priests and presbyterians have the same origin. The Anglo-Saxons also made a new word, now *church*, out of Greek *kyriakon*, 'belonging to the Lord'. The Scots form of the same word, *kirk*, like many other characteristic Scots words distinct from standard English, is not directly descended from the speech of seventh-century Northumbrians who settled in Lothian but from the Danish-influenced form of northern English that came into Scotland with refugees after the Norman conquest of England.

WAUGHTON contains an Old English word *Walh* for a foreigner, especially a Romanised foreigner. The same or related Germanic words give the names to the Welsh, the Walloons of Belgium, perhaps the Valais in Switzerland, and the Vlachs of the Balkans. Unfortunately Waughton or Wauchtoun is not recorded early enough for us to know whether it is an old name referring to a place where native Britons still lived (like many of the Waltons in England) or a later name from a time when Wauch had become a personal name, and thus the settlement of a man called Wauch. The odd shape of the enclosures around the remains of the castle, and indeed the odd shape of the parish that wraps around Waughton, may suggest the older origin.

Gaelic names

There are in East Lothian some transparently Gaelic names, such as Balgone (*baile*, meaning 'settlement'). Drem ('back' or 'ridge') and Gullane ('shoulder') are almost certainly Gaelic though the related Cumbric words would be almost indistinguishable. Others are less well known or less definite. Within our parish, not counting possible candidates among field names, there is one almost definite wholly Gaelic name and one very curious probable instance. As with the Cumbric names early Gaelic names are usually simple geographical descriptions.

The modern CRAUCHIE farm is on low-lying land that would have been very marshy until drained in the last few centuries. However, East Crawho (1822 map) was nearer to Waughton, and thus nearer to the odd rock outcrops, shaped like hay or peat stacks, to the west of the road at Waughton. The name was Crahoc in a document of around 800 years ago, when Gaelic names were relatively new and there may still have been some Gaelic speakers among the more elderly of the nobility in this area. The name may be from *Cruachach*, 'place of stacks', or *Cruachag*, 'little stack'. If it has not migrated from an original reference to the stack-like outcrops, the name may refer to a place where materials were habitually stacked.

The name GILMERton, an estate which formerly included Markle which is within our parish, obviously has an English form and an English ending but probably contains the name of one of the Gaelic speakers who gave such names as Crauchie. For Gilmour is *Gille Moire*, 'servant of Mary', a typical Gaelic Christian name of the twelfth century.

PHANTASSIE has counterparts in the Garleton Hills and near Kirkcaldy in Fife. Unfortunately there are no early spellings. The modern pronunciation and the eighteenth-century spelling - Fancy - tell against a Gaelic origin, though why anyone should name a farm, a house or a hillside from French *Fantaisie* (ultimately from Greek) is difficult to guess. All three Phantassies seem to share the geographical feature of a gentle slope running down to soft ground at its foot. This makes perfect sense of Gaelic *fàn taise*, 'slope of softness'. If this is the origin, the old pronunciation similar to 'Fan Tashie' had been assimilated by the eighteenth century to that of a more familiar word. Curiously, our Phantassie is close to a field formerly named Dysart, a Gaelic borrowing from Latin, and the Phantassie in Fife is not far from the former village of Dysart.

More recent names

Until more whimsical and arbitrary names began to be popular in the eighteenth century, place-names were still usually straightforward records of topography or ownership. Thus SMEATON was *Smetoun*, 'a smith's settlement'; BEANSTON (*Beinstoun*, fourteenth century) 'the settlement of Bein'; and the still remembered GOURLAYBANK and several surviving field names are reminders of the great medieval land-owning de Gourlay family (see Chapter 3). DRYLAWHILL simply describes a place of shallow soils over rock, quick to dry out, CAULDSIDE to the colder, northerly slope of the slight hill at Smeaton, while SUNNYSIDE is on a southerly slope. LAWHEAD is at the top of a hill, while KAMEHILL is shaped something like the kame or crest of a cockerel.

Finally, many names remain obscure, or are ambiguous, especially where they are of minor features and have only been recorded in recent times. Several Old English words were similar and tended to become confused in place-names, so that it is difficult to know whether HAILES is named from aristocratic halls, angles in the course of the Tyne, or patches of flat ground by the river. Is the gully called HOWKINS, south of the castle, so-called because it looks as if it has, in broad Scots, been 'howkit oot'; or could it be a worn down survival of a Cumbric *helygen*, 'place of willows'?

John W. Steele

[8] The thirteenth-century chancel of Preston Kirk.

Chapter 3

MEDIEVAL TIMES

Norman knights and feudalism

The Norman invasion of England in 1066 forced many Anglo-Saxons to flee to Scotland. These included Cospatric, Earl of Northumbria, who was granted Dunbar as part of an extensive estate, and the Saxon Princess, Margaret, who became Malcolm Canmore's second queen in about 1070. Malcolm did his utmost to exploit the situation to his own advantage but in 1093 he was killed near Alnwick, in Northumberland.

David I, the youngest son of Malcolm and Margaret, succeeded to the throne in 1124. His reign was among the most momentous of any Scottish monarch, for it was he who began the process of feudalising the country, a process continued by his two grandsons who succeeded him, Malcolm IV 'the Maiden' and William I 'the Lion'. Although born in Dunfermline, David had been brought up at the court of his brother-in-law, Henry I of England. There he adopted Norman ways and customs, and when he returned home in 1113 he brought with him many of his friends, Bretons and Flemings as well as Normans, who would help him to revolutionise the way Scotland was governed.

These incomers included Walter fitz Alan, of Breton origin, who was given Stenton and Innerwick as part of a vast estate; Walter was given the trusted position of steward in the royal household and his descendants would in time found the Stewart royal dynasty. Another incomer, Alexander de St. Martin, who was granted Athelstaneford and other lands near Haddington, hailed from the hamlet of St Martin, beside Bellencombre in Upper Normandy. The situation in Prestonkirk is not clear but by the reign of William 'the Lion' the lordship of Hailes had been granted to one of the de Gourlay family; the de Gourlays were associated with the more powerful Balliols, who originated in Picardy.

King David and his grandsons revolutionised Scotland. They founded burghs to control trade, such as Haddington where William's son, the future Alexander II, was born in 1198; they minted coins for the first time; they introduced monastic orders, which built great abbeys and priories: they reorganised the Church into dioceses and parishes; and they and their knights built castles from which they could dominate the land. It was said at the time that 'you could'na hear mass being said for the sound of the masons' hammers'.

The parish of Prestonkirk, then called Linton, was established at this time. It lay within the diocese of St. Andrews and the archdeanery of Lothian. The present boundaries are probably not much different from those defined by de Gourlay and the Bishop of St. Andrews over 800 years ago. In addition, de Gourlay would have paid for the building of a fine stone church, the running of which he entrusted to the monks of Kelso Abbey. Nothing of that first Norman building has survived, but the splendid chancel, housing the altar, that was added to the nave in the early thirteenth century and dedicated by Bishop David de Bernham at a service there in 1240, does still stand. Its elegant Gothic windows and buttresses have been described as by far the most worthwhile piece of thirteenth-century architecture in Lothian. The earliest parts of Hailes Castle also date from this time, making it one of the oldest stone castles in Scotland. The de Gourlays probably employed the same masons at both.

The Red Friars at Houston

During the course of the thirteenth century another ecclesiastical building was erected in Linton, a house of Trinitarian Friars (also known as Red Friars). The founders were Christina (died 1269), a daughter of the Frasers of Tweeddale who held land in the Fortune area, and her husband, Robert de Moubray. The Red Friars established their house at Houston ('Hugh's toun'), close by the parish church.

The order had been founded shortly before 1200 at Cerfroy in north-east France. They were formed to assist the ransoming from the Saracens of Christians captured during the Crusades. They wore a red and blue cross on their white habits. Their houses were quite small, consisting of three priest brethren and three lay brethren under the leadership of a prior. Their first house in Scotland was founded around 1240 at Berwick, then the country's main burgh and port. Other cells were built at Dunbar and Dirleton. Such friaries served a variety of purposes, and that at Houston was probably a hospital for travellers using the busy road to England.

The site of the friary is marked by a ruin directly below Preston Kirk, and is further indicated by the existing house names of 'Red Friars' and 'Monks' Orchard' in this location. The endowment of the friary was confirmed by a charter of 1271-72, in the reign of Alexander III, and there is some evidence to show that the King actually visited the site to inspect the progress. The endowment was finally transferred with Papal consent in 1541 to another Red Friars' house in Peebles, by which time there was only one elderly friar left at Houston.

The Wars of Independence

The comparatively stable conditions of the thirteenth century were soon disturbed after the untimely death of Alexander III in 1286, and by the death of his grand-daughter and successor, Margaret 'the Maid of Norway', in 1290. Edward I of England, fresh from his conquest of Wales, came north in 1296, stormed Berwick, slew most of the inhabitants, and defeated the Scots army under John Balliol at Dunbar in August. Many Scots were forced to do homage to the English king, among them Richard, the priest in Prestonhaugh (as the parish was by now called), and Brother John of Houston Friary.

In 1297, after Edward's army withdrew, a resistance movement under William Wallace began to achieve considerable success. Any evidence of Wallace's activities in this area rests with the account of Blind Harry, a popular poet at the court of James IV, some 200 years later. He recounts how Wallace was supported locally by Lauder of Tyninghame and Lyle of Stoneypath, near Garvald, 'that did the country ken, at Linton he came up with twenty men'. The poem goes on to tell how Wallace defeated a superior force near Innerwick under Cospatric, Earl of Dunbar, and pursued him out of Scotland.

In the end Wallace was no match for English might and in 1298 was defeated at Falkirk. But the resistance continued under Robert Bruce. In the next quarter of a century Scots and English armies marched and fought, to the general distress of the population, along roads and tracks on the line of what we know as the A1 and the A68. East Linton must have been an important strategic place in those times with the need for a means to cross the River Tyne in times of high water, but no records remain.

Despite Bruce's victory at Bannockburn in 1314 there remained 14 years of struggle, savagery, heroism and treachery before Edward II was forced by his nobles to acknowledge the independence of Scotland and Bruce as its sovereign King at the Treaty of Northampton in 1328. In 1322, Edward II, still smarting from his defeat at Bannockburn and his subsequent escape to Dunbar through East Linton, came north with a huge army. Bruce responded by laying waste the whole of Lothian with a scorched earth policy, and razing castles to the ground to prevent them being used as English garrisons. It is possible that the castle at Hailes was among his targets given its strategic location beside one of the principal roads from England. The English army sent foragers through the country and returned empty-handed except for one lame cow left at Tranent. Whereupon the English commander, the Earl of Surrey, is said to have remarked: 'This is the dearest beef that ever I saw'. By September of that year Edward was forced to withdraw his starving army to England, no engagement having taken place.

The death of Bruce in 1329 brought about renewed hostilities. By 1333, following the Scottish host's defeat at Halidon Hill, near Berwick, the English took control of the eight southern shires, including Haddingtonshire. In the county only Dunbar Castle held out against the enemy, thanks largely to Black Agnes's heroic acts of defiance. Elsewhere destruction was widespread, including the Franciscan friary and its kirk, 'the Lamp of Lothian', at Haddington, and the Virgin's shrine at Whitekirk, which was pillaged.

[9] Hailes Castle and the River Tyne from Overhailes farm. The central part of the castle complex (centre right in the photograph) was built by the de Gourlays in the thirteenth century; the remainder dates from the rebuilding by the de Hepburns following the Wars of Independence with England in the fourteenth century.

The Battle of Prestonkirk, 1401

In February 1401, in the confusion of Robert III's reign, Henry Hotspur, a Percy and son of the Earl of Northumberland, together with the exiled Earl of Dunbar invaded Scotland with an army reported to be 12,000 strong. They advanced to Papple and then headed towards Linton. The Hepburns' stronghold at Hailes held out, but the villages of Hailes, Traprain and Markle, with their granges, were burnt. The English encamped for the night at Preston, probably making use of Houston Friary. However, on the following morning they were disturbed by the Scottish host, under the command of Archibald, the Master of Douglas, who had marched out from Edinburgh Castle overnight. Seeing them coming over the top of Pencraig, the English 'turned tail and ran', according to Abbot Walter Bower in his *Scotichronicon*, all the way back to Berwick.

Although on this occasion Hailes Castle was not captured, it did fall in 1446 after a long siege by the pro-English Archibald Dunbar, who is reported to have slain 'all that he found therein'.

The Hepburns of Hailes

The lordship of Hailes was held by the de Gourlays until the fourteenth century, when their association with the Balliols led to their downfall. Their forfeited estate was granted by David II to Adam de Hepburn, with Waughton going to his elder brother.

Following the acquisition of Hailes, Adam seems to have set about rebuilding the war-damaged castle. Much of what the visitor sees there today belongs to the later fourteenth and early fifteenth centuries. An English general later called it 'a house of verie good strengthe'. The Hepburns increased their property and influence in the area over the next two centuries, acquiring Beanston, Monkrigg, Humbie, Smeaton and Markle. The *Register of the Great Seal of Scotland* records for the year 1363 the granting by the Earl of March to John Hibburne (Hepburn) 'all lands and tenements of Overmerkille (Markle) and Nethermerkille with their pertinances'.

The Hepburns played an important part in Scottish history. Sir Patrick Hepburn of Hailes and his son fought gallantly at the Battle of Otterburn in 1388 during which the Earl of Douglas defeated Henry Percy of Northumberland. A later Patrick Hepburn was created first Earl of Bothwell for helping King James II to defeat the Black Douglases near

Garry S. Menzies

[10] Inside the courtyard at Hailes Castle. The round-headed doorway was originally a grand window lighting the dais, or upper end of the great hall.

Langholm in 1455. Several Hepburns were priests or ministers of Preston Kirk shortly before and after the Reformation.

Undoubtedly the most famous (or infamous) Hepburn was James, Baron Hailes and the fourth Earl of Bothwell, Mary Queen of Scots' third husband. Born about 1535, probably at Hailes itself, Bothwell was implicated in the murder early in 1567 of Mary's second husband, Lord Darnley. Shortly after, on 15 May, Bothwell married his sovereign. But barely a month later, the couple were parted, Bothwell scurrying from the field at Carberry, near Tranent, leaving his wife to 'face the music' alone. He headed north to Orkney, and thence into exile. After years as a political prisoner of the King of Denmark, he died in Dragsholm Castle, Sjaelland, on 14 April 1578, and his mummified corpse was laid to rest in nearby Faarevejle Church. And there it remains!

With Bothwell's forfeiture in 1567, the castle passed first to the Stewarts and then to the Setons. But these noble families had their country seats elsewhere and the local tenants took over the old halls and chambers both for dwellings and for storage.

Richard Fawcett

[11] The skull of James Hepburn, fourth Earl of Bothwell and third husband of Mary Queen of Scots, in Faarevejle Church, Sjaelland, Denmark.

Prestonkirk in Stewart times

The 300 years of the Stewart dynasty saw many armies pass through the parish. The last army marched by during the 1745 Jacobite uprising which effectively ended the aspirations of the Stewarts to return to the throne of Great Britain.

In 1483, Alexander Stewart, Duke of Albany, the brother of James III, attempted to usurp the throne. He even styled himself Alexander R. In that year, he attacked and seized Waughton, despite the stout resistance of David Hepburn, who remained loyal to the King. In an endeavour to aid France in 1513, James IV crossed the Tweed with a large army. It was a disaster and King James fell on the battlefield of Flodden along with many Scots of all ranks. An indication of how this affected the parish can be seen from the Buchan-Hepburn genealogy written in 1815:

'When the old Church of Preston was lately [1770] taken down Wauchton's aile [the laird of Waughton's private aisle and burial place] was blown up by gunpowder, the walls being very strongly built. A stone much shattered was thrown out bearing an inscription that it was erected in memory of Hepburn of Wauchton, killed at Flodden in 1513. Kentigern Hepburn of Wauchton, Adam Hepburn Earl of Bothwell, Sir Adam Hepburn of Craig and many others of the Hepburn name fell at Flodden'.

Chris Tabraham

[12] The sole surviving stump of masonry at Waughton Castle, once as impressive a castle as Hailes.

One of Prestonkirk's most distinguished residents in Stewart times was Gavin Douglas, third son of Archibald, fifth Earl of Angus ('Bell the Cat'). Born in about 1475, probably at Tantallon Castle, Master Gavin studied at St. Andrews University before entering the priesthood in 1494, as the 'rector of Hauch' and 'person [parson] of Lyntoun'. In 1503 he left the parish to become Provost of St. Giles, in Edinburgh, and in 1516 joined the élite as Bishop of Dunkeld. He died in 1522.

However, it was not as a cleric that he found lasting fame, but as a makar, or poet. His *Eneados*, a translation of Virgil's *Aeneid*, remains a classic to this day. His longest composition, an allegorical poem called *The Palice of Honour*, was probably written during his time at Preston Kirk. It opens with the poet rising early one May morning and entering a delightful garden:

In broider'd beds unnumber'd flowers were seen,
Of Nature's couch the living tapestry;
And, hid within their leafy curtains green,
The little birds pour'd forth such harmony
As fill'd my very heart with joy and glee...

The War of the 'Rough Wooing' and Linton-Briggis

In 1542, James V died 'a broken reed of a man' following his army's defeat at Solway Moss, on the western Border. He left behind him an heir, Mary, just six days old. Henry VIII of England tried again to obtain a dynastic marriage alliance, proposing that his young son, Edward, should be betrothed to Mary. The Scots would have none of it, and so Henry ordered the Earl of Hertford to invade Scotland with a huge army. The destruction wrought by Hertford's men in south-east Scotland in the summer campaigns of 1544 and 1545 came to be known as the War of the 'Rough Wooing'. Abbeys and churches, castles and towers, towns and villages were destroyed, including Markle in 1544.

On Henry's death early in 1547, his son became Edward VI. But the reins of government were in the hands of Hertford, Edward's uncle, who became Duke of Somerset and Lord Protector of England. Somerset was soon back in Scotland, passing through Linton and meeting with little resistance, except from the garrison in Hailes Castle which he avoided by passing over Pencraig. He proceeded by way of Beanston to Pinkie, near Musselburgh, where he defeated a larger Scottish army.

After Pinkie, Somerset set about controlling the country by erecting garrison fortresses, from Roxburgh on the English Border as far north as Broughty Ferry. The chief base was to be at Haddington, the closest to Edinburgh. Early in 1548 he sent a force under the command of Colonel Wilsford, who had been wounded at Pinkie, to erect the artillery fortification at Haddington. Mary of Guise, the Queen Regent, responded by appealing to Henry II of France, and a French force was sent to assist the Scots. It arrived in time to find the English dismantling the fifteenth-century St. Mary's Church, the lofty tower of which, being outside their defences, posed a threat. The English were disturbed in their destruction and retreated inside their defences. So began the siege of Haddington which was to last for 18 months.

The English supply line from Berwick passed through Linton and over the Tyne. In 1547, Somerset wrote of coming to 'a fayre ryver callen Lyn...over this river is ther a stone bridge that they name Lynton brig...Our horsmen and carriages past through the water (for it was not very depe); our footmen over the bridge'.

Linton Bridge was more commonly known then as Linton-Briggis. It was frequently attacked by the Scots and the French, but the English stoutly defended it. However, in September 1549, shortly before the siege of Haddington ended, it was reported in a letter to William Cecil, the English secretary of state, that the French 'have overthrown Lynton Bridge and are rasing [that is, demolishing] it, and entrenching that passage to stop us. We cannot otherwise pass for the abundance of water "as the lyke hath byn seldom sen"'.

Soon afterwards the English garrison in Haddington, faced with starvation and disease, escaped, unnoticed or unhindered, and the siege came to an end. It was one of the longest and most significant in Scottish history. The 450th anniversary of the siege was commemorated in 1998 by a *son et lumière* in St. Mary's Church, Haddington.

The damage to Linton Bridge was evidently repaired, but the work must have been hasty and inadequate. For the next 200 years and more, the various authorities argued over who should pay for a proper repair. In 1619, for example, the Privy Council declared that 'the brig of Lyntoun is now become verrie ruynous and decayit, the pend and pillaris thairof schaikin, and the haill brig to all appeirance lyke verrie scheortlie to fall downe' and ordered that repairs be put in hand. Little seems to have happened as a result and in 1677 tolls were levied on those using the bridge, ostensibly to finance the necessary repairs. These ranged from 2d. for a single horseman and 4d. for a flock of sheep to 6s. 8d. for each millstone carried on a cart drawn by horses. Christopher Sked was appointed the first toll-keeper. So poor was the state of the bridge that a chain was put across it when the river was fordable to prevent carts from crossing over. Eventually the bridge was properly rebuilt - in 1763, over 200 years after the French engineer had laid his powder charge!

Chris Tabraham

[13] Linton Bridge from the Linn Rocks.

Markle Manor

The names of the great and grand abound in the pages of history, but the ordinary folk rarely get a mention. However, in the *Register of the Great Seal* for 1539 we find the earliest record of named inhabitants of the parish. The nine people mentioned were all tenants in Markle, then held of the Earl of Bothwell by Mary Hepburn and her husband, John Carkethill. Each tenant farmed one or two husbandlands (26 Scots acres). Three of those named, Alex Quhite (White), Will Brown and John Dudgeon, have familiar surnames of tenant farmers in the surrounding area over the next three centuries. It would be fascinating to discover how - or indeed if - they and their families survived the 'Rough Wooing' in 1544, during which Markle was destroyed.

Markle is often erroneously called a monastery. The error was made in the nineteenth century when a reference to the collegiate church of St. Mary at Markle was taken as evidence for there having been a monastic house. A chapel called St. Mary's is first mentioned in 1511, and this would have served as the church for the Hepburns of Markle and their tenants, to save them having to go each day to the parish church in Preston; in those days Mass had to be attended daily. There were similar chapels at Hailes and Waughton castles.

From 1515 there are references in the records to a provost and prebendaries (serving priests), indicating that the Hepburns of Markle had chosen to pay for a small college of priests to pray for their souls in the hope that this would enable them to enter Heaven. The field in which the present ruin of Markle stands is still known as Provost's Park but the site of the chapel is not known.

The 1539 charter paints a brief but interesting word-picture of Markle at that date. It is clearly described as 'a manor, surrounded by orchards and gardens, ponds and pools'. The reference to ponds and pools conjures up a picture remarkably like the scene we have today at Markle Fisheries.

The surviving ruin was excavated in 1978 and shown to be a laird's house dating from about 1600. It must therefore have been in this house that one of the most shameful crimes in Prestonkirk's history took place.

The sordid details are given in the records of the Privy Council for 1601, at which date Markle was the property of Robert Hepburn of Alderstoun. Robert, with several others, including George Hepburn of 'Elstaineford', Henry Sinclair of 'Quhytkirk' and George Hepburn of Stevenson, stood accused of forcibly entering at dead of night the house of George Karkettle (presumably a descendant of John Carkethill) at

Monkrigg. There they grabbed John's daughter, and thereafter 'careit hir that nycht to the said Robert Hepburn's place of Markhill...in the said place [she] wes maist schamefullie deflorit and forceit, in sic a abhominable and detestable forme as hes not bene hard of among Christeanes'. All the accused eventually got off without punishment.

In 1726 'a gentlemans hoose called Martle' was described as belonging to Sir Francis Kinloch of Gilmerton. The site, however, goes back much further, possibly beyond the first mention of the place 'Merkshulle' in 1312. Numerous objects have been found at the site over the years, including a quernstone and much medieval pottery. Aerial photographs indicate a substantial settlement, and by 1750 there were still standing 16 houses and crofts on both sides of a street.

John W. Steele

[14] The site of Markle Manor beyond a fish-pond at Markle Fisheries. The ruined building was the laird's manor house, built about 1600.

King Jamie Saxt

Turbulent times continued during the reign of James VI, who succeeded to the throne in 1567, the year James Hepburn, his mother Mary's third husband, fled north away from his family seat at Hailes. King James's troubles came more from religious strife than political problems, for he was determined to establish his authority and enforce Episcopacy on the Reformed Scottish Kirk.

Two incidents involving the parish during his reign are worthy of mention. Firstly, in 1588 preparations were made to defend Scotland against the Spanish Armada. A real threat was believed to exist as the Duke of Guise, a cousin of Mary Queen of Scots, had formed an alliance with Philip of Spain. It was feared that the Armada would land in Scotland in the expectation of support. On the defeat of the Armada, prayers of thanksgiving were said in Preston Kirk by Robert Hepburn, the minister, who had taken a prominent part in the arrangements to counter the invasion. There were frequent musters of armies throughout the Lowlands and fires were lit on the hills, including no doubt Traprain Law.

The second incident, in 1595, involved the King in person. In 1576, Francis Stewart became fifth Earl of Bothwell after his uncle, James Hepburn, had fled Scotland. Francis was the son of Lord John Stewart, Mary Queen of Scots' half-brother, and Lady Jean Hepburn, James's sister. Francis resided chiefly at Crichton Castle, near Pathhead, but he also held Hailes and is said to have played the part of the devil at the witches' coven in North Berwick, which became notorious during the witch-hunts of James's reign. Francis Stewart was a remarkably complex individual, highly talented in many things but also a rampant ruffian. He eventually fell out with James and was pursued by the King in person to East Lothian. During the chase, James's horse stumbled on the banks of the Tyne and the King, heavily armoured, had to be pulled out of the water to prevent him from drowning.

Chapter 4

THE SEVENTEENTH CENTURY: RELIGIOUS STRIFE

Witches

On the death of Elizabeth I of England in 1603, James VI succeeded her as James I of England, thus uniting the two Crowns. He immediately set out for London, and on his way south passed through Linton. The line of the road at that time ran down Pencraig past the standing stone known locally as the 'Long Stane' and by Langside and the Mill Wynd and so over Linton Bridge.

King James was noted, among other things, for inaugurating a concentration on witch-hunting. Indeed, from 1563-1736 there were no fewer than 290 people burned for witchcraft in East Lothian. The true total may be higher as this number is obtained only from the records. There are just two recorded instances in Prestonkirk parish. On 17 September 1649, Janet Nicolson was 'execut and brint at Hailis for witchcraft', while on 13 June 1661, Janet Hog was accused by the minister and elders of Prestonhaugh at Linton, judged guilty of witchcraft and executed.

Covenanting times

In 1619 John Dalzell was appointed minister of Preston Kirk where he remained for the next eventful 50 years. He came from Lanarkshire with a strong Covenanting background. After the accession of Charles I in 1625, Episcopal innovations were being forced on the Kirk. In addition, all grants of land and property made by the Crown since 1542 were revoked. This alienated the nobles and landed proprietors, many of who had acquired these in supporting James VI. Charles, like his father, believed in the Divine Right of Kings, but unlike his father put religion before politics.

In 1637 Dean Hannay of Edinburgh read in St. Giles at the King's command from Archbishop Laud's *Liturgy*, superseding Knox's *Book of Common Order*, and the whole country burst into uproar. Jenny Geddes is reputed to have thrown her creepie stool at Hannay shouting: 'Wha daur say Mass in my lug?'. In February 1638 the National Covenant defending the Protestant religion was signed at Greyfriars in Edinburgh by all classes with great enthusiasm. A month later it was signed publicly by the whole body of parishioners in Preston Kirk. In June a fast was proclaimed and a heart-searching service was conducted which prepared the people for the struggle which was to follow.

John Dalzell attended the General Assembly in Glasgow in November 1638, at which the Marquis of Hamilton, the King's Commissioner, had instructions to thwart the Kirk acting against Episcopacy. However, the Assembly defied the King, uprooted the whole Episcopal system and re-established Presbyterian polity. War between the King and the Covenanters was now inevitable, and both sides made preparation.

Prestonkirk parish became the centre of a military muster for the country. Many who had signed the Covenant, or were ready to stand by it, exhorted by their ministers, assembled on Beanston Muir on 28 March 1639. The East Lothian regiment under the command of the Laird of Waughton marched with the Scottish army to Duns Law where they camped. Every tent carried a flag inscribed 'For Christ, Crown and Covenant'. King Charles with his army came as far as the banks of the Tweed but seeing the numbers and enthusiasm of the Covenanters concluded a treaty of peace.

In 1640 the whole country was again roused to action and the army was reassembled. The East Lothian regiment, again under the Laird of Waughton's command, marched with the rest of the Scottish host into England, accompanied by Mr. Dalzell, the minister of Preston Kirk. On their return in the following year a public thanksgiving service was observed in Preston Kirk.

In 1642 the Solemn League and Covenant bound the Scots to give military assistance to the English Parliamentarians in exchange for safeguarding the Kirk. In support the men of East Lothian once again mustered on Beanston Muir and at Linton Bridge before marching into England. But this departure of the Scots army to England, under General Leslie's command, gave Montrose his opportunity in the north of Scotland. There was great concern when Montrose moved into the south of Scotland and all available men in the parish between 16 and 60 were mustered. Leslie was recalled from England and under his command Montrose was defeated at Philiphaugh, near Selkirk, on 13 September 1645.

Cromwell and Charles II

In 1649, after his defeat in the English Civil War, Charles I was executed by the English Parliamentarians, despite Scottish objection. Cromwell marched north the following year and the parish was again the scene of much military activity with marching and counter-marching of the armies under Cromwell and Leslie. Leslie had the advantage over Cromwell in tactics until a Parliamentary Committee and Ministers overruled him on Doon Hill, near Dunbar, and the army charged down the hill to defeat. The country was then subjected to the rule of Cromwell for the next 10 years. Hailes, and possibly Waughton, were among the many castles destroyed by Cromwell's guns.

The cessation of the state of war which had existed for several years prior to 1650 brought benefit to the countryside and enabled some of Cromwell's officers remaining in East Lothian under General Monck's administration to apply their knowledge of farming gained in East Anglia. One such was Colonel Stanfield who establised sheep rearing and cloth making near Haddington.

Charles II was restored to his throne in 1660. In 1663 the parish biennial visitation took place. Comments were made on the state of the fabric of the church, the absence of communion cups (two new cups were eventually purchased in 1692), the need to remove the school from the church and the poor state of the bell (even though the bell-tower with its new bell had only been added to the medieval church in 1631) .

Two bells were used at funerals in bygone days. The little hand or mort bell was rung by the beadle to notify a death in the parish and sometimes to lead the funeral cortège. The better-off had the 'great' or kirk bell tolled. Costs for bell ringing depended on which bell was used. The money raised went towards the poor of the parish.

'...For great bell and mortcloth to the Lady Smeatoun...£3. 16s.
(Extract from the Kirk Session minutes for 23 May 1708.)

John W. Steele

[15] The 'great' bell hanging in the tower at the west end of Preston Kirk. The bronze bell, still in use, was originally cast in 1631 but recast in 1846.

The debate as to who should rebuild Linton Bridge continued, and an Act of the Privy Council in 1666 acknowledged both its importance to communication between Scotland and England and also its ruinous state. Contributions for its repair were collected from all the churches south of the Forth. Preston Kirk contributed £16.

In 1683-4 other visitations took place which revealed that the poor box was empty and nothing had been done about 'the ruinous fabrick of the church, especially the glass windows which were much broken down by the schollars'. The brethren represented to the minister and heritors how convenient it would be if there were a schoolhouse. At that time the school was held in Bothwell's Aisle in the church.

Conventicles

The persecutions during Charles II's reign affected many in the parish. William Temple of Linton was an ardent Covenanter and one of the leading spirits of a conventicle held in 1678 on Whitekirk Hill attended by more than 1000 people from all parts of East Lothian. The meeting was broken up by the local garrison and during the ensuing scuffle one of the soldiers was killed. Four were arrested, including Temple for being in possession of a sword. One was executed in Edinburgh and Temple was sentenced to transportation to the Virginia plantations to be sold into slavery.

There were numerous other conventicles held in East Lothian, attended by many from Prestonkirk. Many had to flee from their homes and take refuge in the moors and hills. A list of the fugitives in 1684 gives the names of several of these - John Carfrae, servant in Houston; William Yuill, Traprain; John White, chapman (pedlar) in Preston; Archibald, litster (dyer) in Preston; Richard Sheriff, Knowes; George Knox, Lawhead, and William Keel, his servant.

John Dalzell managed to hold on to his ministry at Preston Kirk despite his Covenanting past until 1669. He was succeeded by George Shiels who continued until the Revolution in 1689 when he was deprived of the living for refusing to read the proclamation from the pulpit of the accession of William and Mary and also to pray for the new sovereigns. Shiels, a staunch Episcopalian, is quoted as saying that 'the Pope was as little infallible as the Bishop of the Isles'.

In 1679, Dr. Gilbert Rule, an ardent Presbyterian, was granted permission by the Privy Council to hold a meeting place at Linton Bridge (now Bridgend House) where those who were not of Mr Shiels's Episcopal flock could meet. Dr. Rule was supported by the Earl of Haddington, a signatory to the Covenant. In 1680 he was invited to baptise his niece in St. Giles in Edinburgh, for which he was arrested the next day and brought before the Privy Council in Edinburgh for holding a conventicle outwith his licence at Linton. He was sentenced to imprisonment on the Bass Rock. The King sent his special thanks by letter from Windsor Castle to the Privy Council and ordered the meeting place to be demolished.

Dr. Rule's health suffered from his time on the Bass and he was released under a bond of 5000 merks that he would depart the kingdom (of Scotland) within eight days. He fled to Leyden, in Holland, where he took the degree of Doctor of Medicine, later returning to practise as a physician in Berwick. In 1690, the Acts establishing Episcopacy and royal supremacy were repealed, the Westminster Confession of Faith was ratified, and the Kirk was restored to the legal position of 1592. Dr. Rule was appointed minister of Greyfriars Church in Edinburgh and went on to become Principal of Edinburgh University.

Preston Kirk

The grassy knoll beside the River Tyne on which the present church stands has been a place of worship since at least the twelfth century. Indeed, its origins may go back to the age of St. Baldred, though nothing survives from his time.

The present kirk is substantially the one rebuilt in 1770. It was built over the place where the nave of the medieval church once stood. In the possession of the church are numerous carved stones of fine quality and medieval date indicating that the medieval church was indeed a grand building. Two stones in particular are of fifteenth-century date - one with a carving of an angel and the other bearing a 'green man' - and come from a fine vaulted ceiling, possibly part of a porch added to the nave.

Fortunately, the thirteenth-century chancel did survive the Georgian rebuilding, probably because it had already been appropriated as a private burial-aisle. It is just possible that this was the Bothwell Aisle, the property of the Hepburns of Hailes.

In 1631 the square bell-tower at the west end was added. The bell itself still hangs, though it was recast by the firm of Thomas Mears, of Whitechapel in London, in 1846.

The main body of the church is largely that built in 1770, though it too has been greatly altered down the

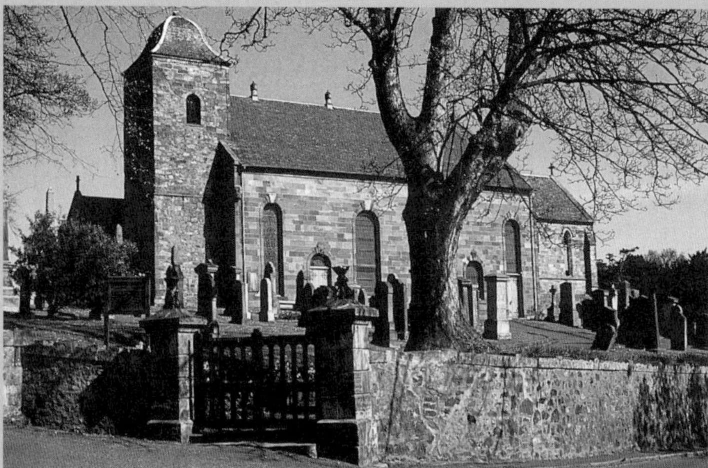

John W. Steele

[16] Preston Kirk from the south. The thirteenth-century chancel is on the right and the seventeenth-century bell-tower on the left.

years. This Georgian kirk originally had timber galleries around three sides of the interior with the minister's canopied pulpit centrally placed along the south wall. There were box-pews providing seating for 600 souls.

The rising population of the parish, however, soon called for an enlargement of the kirk. In 1824 the north wall was taken down and rebuilt 3m further north and the number of seats increased to 800. Signs of that extension can be seen on the east and west outside walls.

In 1891-2 a major refurbishment was undertaken by the architect, James Jerdan. New tall windows replaced the old double-row arrangement. Internally, the galleries and box-pews were removed, and interest was concentrated at the western end where an arcaded Jacobean-style screen, with the pulpit in the centre, was erected. An organ was inserted into the screen shortly afterwards, and more recently, in 1997, the stained-glass memorial windows from St Andrew's Church were transferred to Preston Kirk following the sale of the former Free Church.

John W. Steele

[17] The 'green man' ceiling boss.

After the Revolution of 1689 there was a short ministry in Preston Kirk by John Harvie before his death in 1691. He was followed by John Forrest, a staunch Presbyterian. The oldest existing Session minute book began at the start of his ministry in 1692.

In that year it is recorded that 'Each Lord's day the two elders who collect the public collection shall go through the toun of Linton after sermon begins and also after both sermons to see if any abuse be there by untimeous excessive drinking, and inform the Minister or Session thereof'. Keeping the sabbath was evidently of paramount importance in those days as William Little, a wright in Markle, and his spouse, Sarah Rig, found to their cost in 1709 when they were accused of breaching the Lord's Day 'for making a chest to the deceased child of Patrick Hepburn of Beanstoun, without any necessity'; both expressed their sorrow for the sin, were rebuked and dismissed.

Around this time we read of the minister complaining 'that many folk made a great disturbance in the kirk by going out before the blessing; therefore orders that the north door be lockit by the officer till efter the blessing, and that he stand at one door, and his son at another, and suffer none to go out until the blessing is said'.

At that time the church had an earthen floor with flagstones laid irregularly in the passages so that difficulty was experienced in getting the communion table to stand securely. Each worshipper had to bring their own seat, or erect a permanent one on the approval of the Kirk Session. In 1693, for example, Thomas Thomson in Hailes was given permission by the Kirk Session to 'set a seat for his wife in some convenient place in the church' so long as it was located in 'some fit place where it will not be in any way prejudicial'. The roof was probably thatched and a turf dyke surrounded the building. In 1694 it was resolved to lay the flagstones properly in consequence of the trouble with the communion table. In 1697 it is recorded that 'damage to the roof of the church finally persuaded the Session that the kirk, manse, bell tower and glass windows should be repaired'.

Chapter 5

THE EIGHTEENTH CENTURY: AGRICULTURAL REVOLUTION

National and local concerns

The new century dawned with the inhabitants of Linton and Prestonkirk concerned about both local and national affairs, for these were stirring times. The minutes of the Kirk Session show that the parishioners' attentions were focused on such weighty matters of national importance as Marlborough's victories over the French and Bavarians, and on the proposed Union of the Parliaments of Scotland and England, which came about in 1707. A public fast was observed, and opposition to the Union was led by Lord Belhaven and Andrew Fletcher of Saltoun, near neighbours of the parish.

Meanwhile, local issues of concern included the future of the parish school and the perennial problem of the state of Linton Bridge. In 1703, Thomas Findlay, the minister, reported to the Session that the bridge has been repaired at a cost of '£9.13s.8d. (Scots) which sum the Session appointed their treasurer to pay'. Despite this, the bridge continued to be used when it shouldn't have been. On 27 May 1711 the Session was informed that 'James Dods, smith in Linton, had been guilty of a horrid profanation of the Lord's day, by mending the stage coach, last Lord's day in the time of divine worship, which was broken by being driven violently over the chain when the water was fordable, and so had done a great dale of damage to the bridge'.

Jacobites and Hanoverians

Mr. Matthew Reid was minister during what proved to be the final Jacobite uprising in 1745-6. He would have seen his parish as a busy place before and after the battle of Prestonpans, which was fought on 21

September 1745. Dr. Alexander (Jupiter) Carlyle, afterwards minister of Inveresk, then a student who had joined a company of volunteers, records a visit he made on his way to join General Cope, commander of the Hanoverian army, at Dunbar.

On arrival at the camp west of Dunbar late at night, Carlyle could find no place to stay, so he retraced his steps to Prestonkirk and at 2 a.m. knocked up Mr. Reid at his manse. The minister, taking him for a marauder, kept him waiting an hour at the door. The next day Carlyle joined Cope's march to Haddington. After the battle, which Cope lost in 10 minutes flat, the General beat a hasty retreat through Linton on his way back to Dunbar.

According to Carlyle, 'Many people in East Lothian at that time were Jacobites..., the common people in general, as well as two-thirds of the gentry had no aversion to the family of Stuart, and, could their religion have been secured, would have been very glad to see them on the throne again'.

Roads to peace and opportunity

After the collapse of the '45, the constant warfare that had bedevilled the parish for the best part of 500 years ceased, and great opportunities opened up to exploit the talents of the people and the natural resources of the land. The establishment of peace at home and the freer contacts with the outside world laid the foundations of the Scottish Enlightenment, the great flourishing of the arts and sciences which was to continue well into the next century.

One major improvement affecting Linton after the '45 was the development of the road network. During the Jacobite troubles, the Government had realised that the movement of troops had been affected by the bad state of the roads. The passing of the Turnpike Act in 1750 enabled Linton to share in the benefits better communication brought. Chief among them was the formation of the Great Post Road from Dunbar to East Linton, following the old road, and a new road from East Linton to Haddington.

Before Linton Bridge was built in the sixteenth century the old route from the west had come from Beanston down Pencraig to a ford on the Tyne near Hailes Castle. This was inconvenient in time of flood so when Linton Bridge was built a road was made from Pencraig into Linton via Langside, enabling the Tyne to be crossed by the bridge. A ford was situated above the bridge, about midway between the railway and A1 bridges, and a gap between nos. 5 and 6 Lauder Place indicates the approach-road to it. A large stone, the 'Jook Stane' (Duck Stone), once lay in the river-bed at that point and served to indicate the depth of water; it was washed away in the great flood of 1948. A right of way, Longstone, still exists along the Langside route. This continued to be the only road until the Post Road (the present A1) was built in 1751.

The Post Road enabled produce to be moved to the markets and the speed of communications to be greatly increased. Coaches on their way between Edinburgh and London passed through the town, and Linton became a staging post where the horses were changed, probably at the Douglas Inn, near where Torness Motors' office now stands.

Before 1750 all the roads of the district were repaired under the provision of the General Statute Labour Act of Scotland whereby each year every tenant was bound to work six days with his horses and carts, and every householder to perform six days' service towards the repair of the public roads. The Act proved unworkable and the Turnpike Act enabled the erection of the Post Road, managed by Trustees who could levy tolls to pay for repairs and maintenance. A toll-house still stands in Lauder Place on the east side of Linton Bridge.

An agricultural revolution

Although the pre-Reformation monks may have been good husbandmen, the knowledge and practice of agriculture was in a poor state in Scotland after five centuries of successive wars. Improvements were becoming evident by the middle of the eighteenth century, following the experiences of those like Cockburn of Ormiston who had travelled south to attend the new British Parliament after the Union of 1707. Seeing new farming practices, they returned home bringing the innovations with them. Cockburn himself introduced the humble turnip to the county, which enabled cattle to be kept during the winter, so providing fresh meat and manure. Potatoes were grown for feeding pigs and new varieties of grain appeared.

Because many of the lairds were engaged in government or the law, they looked for good tenants to manage their estates during their absence. One such laird was George Buchan-Hepburn, a lawyer, who at the end of the century became a Baron of the Exchequer and a Baronet. He built Smeaton House in 1790 and wrote on agricultural affairs. Most lairds had the foresight to grant long leases to their tenants. This unique advantage gave the tenants the incentive, which previously did not exist, to improve both land and buildings.

As the century progressed dramatic agricultural improvements were introduced. These included a new type of swing plough, the brainchild of James Small, of Rosebank near Dalkeith, which with its iron head and mould-board was capable of being drawn by just two horses rather than four. His plough was in wide use by 1782, and innovations like this enabled more and more land to be cultivated. The outfield, often more than half the land, which had hitherto been used for grazing, was cleared of scrub, drained and brought under the plough.

The importance of adding lime to the land became more fully appreciated and bigger and better lime-kilns were built. That built by George Rennie of Phantassie to the south of the A1, which still stands, was among the earliest in the country. The small farming communities with their rigs and outfields gave way to enclosed single farms rented to one tenant, and the dispossessed farmers became farm servants.

Chris Tabraham

[18] George Rennie's limekiln beside the road to Stenton.

By the close of the century, all this enterprise and endeavour had transformed

East Lothian from a county lagging behind the better farming areas of England to one in the lead, attracting international recognition. The new detached farmhouses at, for example, Drylawhill and Overhailes reflect this prosperity; formerly the farmer's dwelling had usually been part of the steading. Another sign of prosperity was the orangery built beside Beanston farmhouse. George Buchan-Hepburn's *General Agricultural View of East Lothian*, published in 1794, described the enormous advances that had been made in agricultural knowledge. Three men from the parish played a leading part in that revolution - Meikle, Rennie and Brown.

Meikle, Rennie and Brown

ANDREW MEIKLE OF HOUSTON MILL

The need to thresh the greatly increased amount of grain now being produced required a more efficient method than the old flail. This problem was successfully met by Andrew Meikle's invention - a machine with beaters, scutchers, rakes, shakers and fanners. The processes of threshing, shaking and winnowing were all performed by the same piece of machinery, and his concept continues to beat at the heart of the combine-harvesters of today.

Andrew Meikle, born in 1719, was brought up on the Fletcher estate at Saltoun. His father, James, had been sent to Rotterdam to discover how the Dutch stripped the husks from barley. He is said to have learned the closely-guarded secret by marrying the miller's daughter! Andrew saw this technique used exclusively at Saltoun Mill, and when he moved to Houston Mill, on the Phantassie estate of the Rennies, as civil engineer and millwright, he set about perfecting the invention.

George Rennie, farmer in Phantassie, encouraged Meikle in his work and in 1788 helped him to obtain a patent for his invention. It soon became widely used, driven either by wind-power, water-power or horses; later on it used James Watt's steam-engine. Rennie was among the first to install the new-fangled threshing machine at his farm, driven at first by horses and later by a powerful windmill. The windmill appears in an old engraving, standing near Phantassie House.

Meikle also made improvements to the design of windmills. He was also a fine performer on the lowland pipes. He died at Houston Mill in 1811 at the ripe old age of 92, and was buried in Preston Kirk churchyard. His tombstone, with its eloquent inscription written by his friend, George Rennie, can still be seen close beside the kirk door.

GEORGE RENNIE OF PHANTASSIE

George Rennie was born at Phantassie in 1748, the son of a tenant farmer. He took charge of Phantassie at an early age, on the death of his father, and before long was in a position to be able to purchase the farm from the Countess of Aberdeen. He erected a kiln on his land for burning limestone and showed the benefit of this in heavier crop yields. He made turnips a special crop, and became a successful cattle breeder, gaining prizes at the Highland and Haddingtonshire shows. In 1806 he formed and planted Linton Orchard on the fine south-facing slope reaching down to the Tyne, opposite the Braeheads.

The widespread interest in farming improvements at that time was evident from the number of visits made to Phantassie by leading agriculturalists. They came from England and Ireland, as well as from other European countries; one visitor to Phantassie later became Tsar of Russia! As a result, Scottish farmers were sent to Poland to introduce the new methods and to encourage the use of the swing-plough.

[19] Phantassie farmhouse, steading and windmill in George Rennie's time, by E. M. Wimperis after a drawing by J. S. Miles

But this was not the full extent of Rennie's entrepreneurial skills. With partners he developed the Linton Distillery, started by his father, beside the River Tyne, on the site where the

Free Church Manse (now Manseford) was built in 1847. It became the biggest of nine distilleries in the county and consumed large quantities of Lothian and Berwickshire barley. Water was led through a stone underground duct from a small loch near Pencraig. Much of the whisky was transported to London. The distillery finally closed in 1842.

As a Justice of the Peace, Rennie, aided by Bailie Ballantyne, baker at Bridgend (now the Old Bakehouse), tried to keep order during the harvest season when a large number of itinerant workers were hired. Frequent riots and disturbances took place, especially when Linton whisky began to take effect. Very often Ralph Plain, the village constable, had to bind the ringleaders hand and foot and despatch them to Haddington jail in carts. In one fracas Ralph almost lost his nose!

George Rennie passed away in 1828, aged 79, and he too was buried in the churchyard, to the east of the kirk. The fullsome inscription on his tombstone was composed by his friend, Robert Brown of Markle.

ROBERT BROWN OF MARKLE

Robert Brown was born into an old Linton family in 1756. He farmed first at West Fortune, then at Markle and finally at Drylawhill. While Rennie's work had to be viewed at the time, Brown disseminated the advancing scientific knowledge of agriculture through his writings and as editor of *The Farmers' Magazine*. He established the magazine in 1800 and continued as its editor for the next 14 years. In its pages every aspect of agricultural and rural affairs, including law and politics, was discussed. His writings were translated into French and German and his *Treatise on Rural Affairs* became a standard reference for many years; it was said that it was as widely read as the Bible. A sign of the respect in which he was held came when he received a commission to conduct an extensive survey of the West Riding of Yorkshire, part of the Government's efforts to increase the nation's wealth by improving land-use.

Robert Brown died at Drylawhill in 1831, aged 74, and he too lies in the graveyard, not far from Rennie's lair, where his gravestone can be seen. Brown's Place is named after him.

Preston Mill and Phantassie Doocot

East Linton is famous as much for Preston Mill as for anything else. In its beautiful riverside setting of trees and meadows, with its pantiled roofs, cowled kiln and massive wheel scattering drops of water, the old mill by the stream has attracted generations of artists, photographers and visitors. The precise date of the building may never be known, but that somehow seems irrelevant, for the mill has a timeless quality about it.

There is mention of a mill at Preston in 1599. It was one of many that have been built along the sinuous length of the Tyne down the centuries, all of them drawing off its gushing waters to power machinery for some purpose or another. Preston Mill was a grain mill, processing farm produce for human consumption. Other mills, like that at Houston, directly across the river from Preston (referred to in 1585), and another at Hailes (recorded in 1565), began life as waulk mills, pummelling soaked fibres into a matted cloth. They later became grain mills also. There were other mills in the parish - at Beanston, Monksmill and Linton.

Part of the present structure at Preston Mill may date back to the seventeenth century, and the masonry reveals at least four stages of building. At some stage, the building was raised to house additional machinery and there are indications on the gable supporting the mill-wheel that the added masonry came from the demolition of the main part of Preston Kirk in 1770. The waterwheel and mill machinery date from the later nineteenth and early twentieth centuries.

Sir George Buchan-Hepburn of Smeaton, the owner of the mill, described in 1794 the system of 'thirlage' whereby tenants were obliged to support a mill with its maintenance by taking their grain there to be ground, handing over an agreed portion as payment. This system of imposed thirlage had died out at Preston Mill during the eighteenth century and the mill became a wholly commercial enterprise without the support of a captive market. It was one of the few mills to continue operating well into the twentieth century. Three families - the Watts, the Draffans and George Denholm - had worked it since the 1880s. During the great flood of 1948, the Tyne rose to the level of the top of the front door and caused extensive damage to the vulnerable wooden fixtures and fittings. On 1 January 1950, the mill was gifted to The National Trust for Scotland by the Trustees of the late Mr John R. Gray of Smeaton and extensive renovations have since been carried out.

John W. Steele

[20] Preston Mill from the south.

[21] Phantassie Doocot, on the south of the River Tyne opposite Preston Mill. The doocot, one of four pigeon houses remaining in the parish (the other three are at Drylawhill, Waughton Castle and Hailes Castle), was built in the sixteenth century to provide a ready source of food for the laird of Phantassie's table during the long winter months. It was gifted to The National Trust for Scotland by William Hamilton, farmer in Phantassie, in 1961.

Garry S. Menzies

In 1793, the minister, Mr. Daniel McQueen, penned his contribution to the *Statistical Account of Scotland*, a detailed description of all the parishes in the land. It was the first such account (hence its description 'old'); a second or 'new' account followed in 1845, and a third in 1953 compiled jointly by the Rev. R. R. Fisher and Provost A. P. McCall. Mr. McQueen's account provides a wonderful snap-shot of life and conditions in Linton and the surrounding farms as the century drew to a close.

The population in 1793 stood at 1176, a decrease of 142 since 1755. The 5000 acres of land was growing oats, wheat, pease and beans, barley, potatoes and turnips - in that order of magnitude. Although the church was new (it had been substantially rebuilt in 1770), the manse was old and in bad repair. His plea clearly had the desired effect, for a new manse was built in the following year! Finally, Mr. McQueen describes his parishioners as 'in general industrious and contented with their lot'.

Within two years of McQueen's account, another church appeared in Linton - the United Presbyterian Church in Tyne Close (in use since 1934 as the Masonic Hall). Its first minister was Dr. Hugh Jamieson, who also held a school in his manse at the corner of Brown's Place and Langside.

John W. Steele

[22] The portrait of Dr. Hugh Jamieson, now hanging in the gallery of Preston Kirk.

John W. Steele

[C1] *Traprain Law from Pencraig*

National Museums of Scotland

[C2] *The Traprain Treasure*

Private Collection

[C3] Robert Hope, Church of the Willows, Prestonkirk

Garry S. Menzies

[C4] Detail from Memorial Window, Preston Kirk

Garry S. Menzies

[C5] Margrat Mille's gravestone, 1685, Preston Kirk's oldest memorial

Roger Durman

[C6] Robert Noble, Sketch of Preston Mill

Garry S. Menzies

[C7] Andrew Meikle's headstone, 1811

Private Collection, courtesy of Bourne Fine Art, Edinburgh

[C8] *William Miller Frazer,* On the Tyne

The Scottish National Portrait Gallery

[C9] *John Rennie,*
by Henry Raeburn

Private Collection

[C10] James Paterson, Dusk, East Linton

John W. Steele

[C11] The 'Long Stane' and East Linton

[C12] Robert Noble, East Linton at Dusk

East Lothian Council

East Lothian Council

[C13] *John P. Nicolson,* On the Tyne, East Linton

Roger Durman

[C14] *High Street and St. Andrew's Church*

Chapter 6

THE NINETEENTH CENTURY: CHANGING TIMES

Farming's fickle fortunes

The increase in population and the fall in imports caused by the Napoleonic Wars accelerated the need to increase food production. Yet more land was brought under the plough. As the price of grain rose, so the tenant farmers thrived, and the building of more fine detached farm houses, like Brownrigg, Crauchie, Markle Mains, Preston Mains and Traprain, is evidence of this. Existing homes, like Beanston, and Phantassie, were extended.

After Napoleon's defeat in 1815, the prosperity of the parish's farmers fluctuated throughout the rest of the century. In that year the Corn Law Act was passed which banned the importing of grain below a fixed price. But the demands of the growing population together with the availability of wheat from the Baltic and America gave rise to pressure from industrial interests for cheaper bread to feed the increasing number of factory workers in the cities and towns. In 1845 the fierce debate came to a head with the failure of the Irish potato crop, and Peel's government repealed the Act in the following year.

The price of grain immediately began to fluctuate, to the extent that some tenant farmers departed the parish, to be replaced by farmers from further west. But these changes were gradual and less marked than the effect of the arrival of large quantities of grain from the 'bread baskets' of the American mid-West in 1879. Landlords and tenants were equally hard hit, and some sold out to prosperous merchants from the cities.

Smeaton estate

The century saw the building of many of East Lothian's fine mansion houses. Prestonkirk was graced with Smeaton, among the first to be built, in 1790. It was the home of the parish's only resident heritor, Sir George Buchan-Hepburn (1739-1819). Sir George's father, John Buchan, of Letham near Haddington, had married Elizabeth, the daughter of Patrick Hepburn of Smeaton - and the family name thereafter became Buchan-Hepburn.

Stewart Stenhouse

[23] Smeaton House.

Sir George, created a baronet in 1815, not only built the fine Georgian house (demolished in 1949) but also laid out a fine estate. His grandson, Sir Thomas (1804-1893), who succeeded in 1833 and represented the county in Parliament from 1838 to 1847, also took a keen interest in gardening. He was particularly noted for his tree planting. Most of the large conifers and deciduous trees in the grounds of Smeaton, particularly those around the lake, were planted by Sir Thomas and cared for by his gardener, John Black. John Black came to Smeaton in 1860 and remained head gardener for 50 years. The estate books show that the seeds from which the trees were grown were obtained from pioneer plant collectors returning from remote parts of the world.

John Rennie of Phantassie, civil engineer

Arguably the most famous of Prestonkirk's sons was John Rennie, the civil engineer. Rennie was born at Phantassie on 7 June 1761, the youngest of nine children of James Rennie (including brother George). He attended the parish school and then at the age of 12 was officially apprenticed to Andrew Meikle at Houston Mill, before moving on to Dunbar High School. Returning to Meikle's workshop once more, he began to design his own machinery, and Knowes Mill, at the eastern edge of the parish, was probably his first 'commission'. By 1780 he was fitting up mills as far afield as Invergowrie, in Angus.

In November 1780, Rennie embarked on a degree course at Edinburgh University, where he studied under Professors John Robison and Joseph Black. But in 1783, before he had completed his degree course, he opted to seek his fortune elsewhere and left for London where he was taken on by the firm of Boulton and Watt, designing flour machinery. From there he progressed to designing bridges, canals, land-drainage schemes, docks and harbours.

John Rennie's designs were remarkable for their beauty as well as for their sound construction. Among his many achievements were the Southwark, Waterloo and London bridges across the Thames, dockyards in London, Portsmouth, Chatham and Leith, harbours from Wick to Plymouth, including his famous Plymouth breakwater, and the Crinan and Kennet and Avon canals. So revolutionary were his bridge designs (which, with their innovative elliptical arches, were notable for the absence of a hump-backed appearance) that at the formal opening of the Musselburgh bridge in 1806, the Provost declared that it was 'Nae brig at a'. Ye dinnae ken when you're on it or aff it!'.

When Rennie died in 1821, so famous had he become that his body was not returned to the family lair in Preston Kirk graveyard but instead laid to rest in St. Paul's Cathedral, London. However, in recognition of Prestonkirk's most famous son, a memorial and seat were erected by public subscription in 1936 - 115 years after his death! - beside the by-pass road (it was relocated beside the boundary wall of Phantassie in 1981). The stone pillar in the centre of the platform is a baluster from Rennie's Waterloo Bridge.

[24] The bronze image of John Rennie from his memorial near the A1.

A new Statistical Account

In 1835, the Rev. James Thomson, the Church of Scotland minister, aided by his son and assistant minister, John, wrote a second description of the parish of 'Prestonhaugh, otherwise called Prestonkirk'; it was published in 1845 as part of the *New Statistical Account of Scotland*. He reported on such diverse topics as topography, natural and civil history, population, industry and economy. Among his many fascinating observations is the fact that the 'passage' through the rocky linn - 'The Jaws' - had been blasted through by man earlier in the century to allow sea trout to gain the upper reaches of the Tyne to spawn. Incidentally, the saucer-like holes gouged out of the rock beside the Jaws were lint holes used by the womenfolk when steeping their linen.

Forty years had passed since the Rev. McQueen's first account. During that time the population had grown by almost 600 souls, from 1176 to 1765. Of that number, 715 resided in Linton itself, 48 in Preston and the remainder in the 'country part'. The total had in fact been higher, for in 1821 the number recorded was 1812. The Rev. Thomson put the slight reduction of 47 down to two factors - firstly, the uniting of two or more farms and the consequent pulling down of labourers' houses no longer required; secondly the closure of the United Presbyterian Church's academy and the departure of its 12 or so pupils.

In 1835, the Mill Wynd housed about 100 people. Most worked in the grain mills beside the linn (one a flour mill, the other a barley mill) as well as in the distillery. Fifty folk were employed in Rennie's distillery alone, producing 500,000 gallons of whisky each year. The Rev. Thomson passed no comment on this alcoholic endeavour, but made no secret of his profound dislike of the 11 ale-houses in the parish. These certainly included the Crown Hotel and the Railway Hotel (now the Drovers Inn), and probably also the Golden Lion Hotel (later the Red Lion, and now the Bridgend Hotel). In his view they all had a 'very mischievous effect on the morals of the people, especially of young unmarried men'. The only good word he could find on the subject was the fact that the number had declined from the previous high of 19!

Private Collection

[25] An old postcard dated 1906 showing the complex of mills at the Linn Rocks.

Despite these complaints, the minister wrote of the general exemplary moral behaviour of the people, 'There being no instance within the memory of the writer of any person connected with the parish being convicted of any crime before the Justiciary Court'. According to the police records of Haddington, the most common offences dealt with by the Justices of the Peace in those days were the 'furious driving of carts', followed by 'leaving carts unattended'.

A grave-robbing incident

The village policeman during the Rev. Thomson's day was Ralph Plain. More used to controlling riots during hiring fairs, he was involved in one particularly bizarre criminal episode that occurred about 1830.

The sexton at Preston Kirk was digging a grave for a young woman when a strange man appeared. He asked questions about the deceased and the time of the funeral, before departing. Shortly afterwards, Sir John Buchan-Hepburn of Smeaton received information that the kirkyard was to be raided on a certain night. It was, therefore, agreed that three parties should be posted to await the visitors. One was to hide inside the church, another in the watch-house (built a short time before for keeping guard at the entrance to the kirkyard), and the third, under the charge of Ralph Plain armed with a pistol, among the bushes in the Manse garden.

After a long wait a vehicle with wheels muffled drew up at the church gate, the occupants unloaded their picks and shovels and then made a thorough search of the yard, passing round the church and peering through the windows. This enabled the sexton to identify the face of the man who had shown interest in the grave.

The falling of an oak staff inside the church caused the visitors to rush for the gate, but when all seemed quiet they resumed their activities and soon had the coffin exposed. On a signal from Ralph Plain's pistol the watchers rushed out and seized the body-snatchers, binding them with ropes and conveying them to the laird at Smeaton, the local magistrate, for due processing of the law.

The watch-house at the south end of the Stables is still in use today as a store, but no longer requires to be manned. Ralph Plain's tombstone (he died in 1832) lies close by. Ironically, Dr. Knox, the Professor of Anatomy in Edinburgh University, who encouraged this detested trade in body-snatching, when he was forced to flee the city, took refuge at Holanside, a little farm near Traprain Law. He eventually emigrated to Australia.

'East' Linton and the industrial revolution

In his account of the parish, the Rev. Thomson alluded to the recent erection of steam engines on three (unnamed) farms in the parish 'for the purpose of driving thrashing machines'. The first had appeared in 1828. Steam was the power behind the industrial revolution, but although it had first appeared in 1712, with Newcomen's invention, the replacement of wind, water and animal power had not happened overnight. The tall red-brick chimneys still towering above the steadings at Beanston, Sunnyside and Luggate are reminders of this 'age of steam'.

The appearance of static steam engines in the parish was soon followed by moving ones with the opening in June 1846 of the North British Railway Company's line linking Edinburgh and Berwick. The

[26] The pretty steading at Sunnyside farm. The chimney vented gases from the steam engine which helped thresh the corn.

link to London was completed the following year when Queen Victoria opened the Royal Border Bridge across the Tweed at Berwick. A planned branch line, the East Lothian and Tyne Valley Railway, which was intended to run from Linton via Haddington to Ormiston and Dalkeith, never got beyond the drawing board.

Another failure was the railway bridge across the Tyne which was swept away by a great flood within three months of opening. The story goes that Bailie Ballantyne, the baker at Bridgend and a fine angler, was standing on the old stone bridge when someone called to him to leave the bridge at once for it would soon fall. The Bailie stood his ground and boldly replied: 'Linton Brig fa' doun, ye idiot? Linton Brig will stand for evermore.' He was proved right. The railway bridge was soon rebuilt and remains in use. Not so the railway station, built beside the dower house of Phantassie (now Station House) which the North British Railway Company bought from the Rennies of Phantassie and converted into the booking office and a house for the station-master.

However, before the station was closed in 1963, a casualty of 'Lord Beeching's axe', it had some memorable moments. A. J. Balfour, of Whittingehame House, was often to be seen taking the train for London and the Houses of Parliament (he was Prime Minister from 1902 to 1905). Another distinguished gentleman to alight from the train was Major-General Baden Powell, 'the hero of Mafeking', on the afternoon of Wednesday 11 September 1901, en route for Newbyth House. 'The station platform and grounds were packed with people all eager to get a glimpse of the General', reported the *Haddingtonshire Courier*. 'On his descent from the train, he was greeted with loud and prolonged cheers, the distinguished officer recognising the honour paid him by lifting his cap. He was met at the station by Miss Baird, who drove him to Newbyth.'

The arrival of the railway coincided with another change - the renaming of Linton as 'East' Linton, to distinguish it from another Linton, in Peeblesshire, which became 'West' Linton. Clearly, letters had been going astray following the introduction of Sir Rowland Hill's 'penny post' in 1840. (A Victorian post box still survives set into McArthur's joinery premises at no.1 Bridge End.)

Linton traders

The person in charge of East Linton's Post Office at this date was Alexander Shiells. His premises were beside the Crown Hotel, and he is among a host of traders and merchants then serving the growing population mentioned in the *Haddington Register and Almanac* for 1843.

Tradesmen included James Hardie, joiner; Andrew Hume, cooper; Alexander Smellie, slater; Thomas Smellie, carter; and Francis Storie, farrier. Among the merchants were John Watt, brewer; Robert 'Bailie' Ballantyne, baker; Robert Craies and Robert Shirriff, shoemakers; Thomas Muir, meal-dealer; Greive Smellie, innkeeper of the Crown Hotel; and George Smellie, grocer. Following Ralph Plain's death in 1832, the district constable was William Forrest. The Member of Parliament was Sir Thomas Buchan-Hepburn - who else!

The *Almanac* contains other absorbing snippets of information. There were five public coaches a day - the Royal Mail Coach (the London Mail), the Union Coach, Steel's Defiance Coach, Steel's

Afternoon Coach and the Berwick Coach. These changed their horses at the Douglas Inn, opposite the distillery. The Sacramental Fast Day was held on the Thursday before the third Sunday in July - apparently!

George Laing

[27] A bill-head of George Smellie's grocery business, dated 1880. The premises, at the junction of The Square and Bridge Street, is still a grocer's shop.

Disruption in the Church

The continuing increase in the population, coupled with the widespread practice of church attendance, gave rise to overcrowding in Preston Kirk on Sundays. In 1824, the local building firm, W. & J. Lamb, were engaged in extending the size of the kirk by a third. They had previously (1812) built a new parochial school, and were subsequently contracted in 1832 to build a cholera hospital at Drylawhill (on The Common) and to make alterations to the manse in 1843.

But no sooner had those alterations to the manse been completed than the minister, the Rev. John Thomson, who had succeeded his father, James, in 1841, felt compelled to leave. The main reason behind his going was the reluctance of the Church of Scotland to depart from the traditional system of patronage, especially regarding the choice of ministers, which led to the Disruption of that Church in May 1843 and the formation of the Free Church. (This was a second disruption in the Church of Scotland for an earlier break-away about 1770 had led to the creation eventually of the United Presbyterian (U.P.) Church.) John Thomson, along with many of his colleagues, 'came out' of his church and manse in protest and formed a congregation of the Free Church in East Linton. A large part of his flock followed him westward along Preston Road. By November, their new church, St. Andrew's, was opened, free from debt - testimony to their deep conviction and determination. This speedy work was made possible by far-seeing people who had procured the site beforehand, and by the keen co-operation of the tradesmen and the enthusiasm of voluntary helpers. Other like-minded folk from neighbouring parishes soon joined them to form the new congregation. As if that task was not enough, the congregation had provided a new manse (now Manseford) for the Rev. Thomson by 1847, built on the site of the former distillery!

In response to the growing population of East Linton, St. Andrew's was extended in 1857, and again in 1880 when the present frontage with its attractive helmed spire was built. (The join between the old and the new building is clearly seen along the exterior walls.) So popular did the Free Church become that a second minister, Thomas Adamson, was taken on in 1876; Scotscraig, the fine Late Victorian residence at the Braeheads, was built as the second manse.

Chris Tabraham

[28] 'Jessie' the town clock in the spire of St. Andrew's Church

In 1886, the appearance of the church itself was much improved when some cottages and a stable at the top of Mill Wynd were purchased by the congregation and demolished. A year later, to commemorate Queen Victoria's Golden Jubilee, the Town Council requested permission to put a clock in the tower and the money - £116 - was raised by public subscription. 'Jessie' the clock was formally inaugurated on 31 March 1888. A song, to the tune of *Scots Wha Hae*, composed by James Lumsden (alias Samuel Mucklebackit), the author and poet whose family farmed at Nether Hailes, was sung by James Pettigrew to mark the event. The opening verse ran:

Now's the day and now's the hour,
See our Town Clock in her tower!
Hear her toll the time wi' power,
And melodiouslie!

John W. Steele

[29] A view looking north over Linton bridge towards 'Jessie' the town clock, around 1885. In the foreground is Laing's builder's yard, and just beyond the bridge Fraser's joinery premises (now McArthur's). The fine three-storeyed building is the Red Lion Inn (now the Bridgend Hotel).

'Jessie' was named after Jessie Cowe, the daughter of William Cowe, the local butcher whose business was in The Square. The clock is generally thought to have been unofficially christened by a group of young men who kept East Linton lively at that time. They got together with

Bob, the son of Robert Sharp, the proprietor of the Railway Hotel (now the Drovers Inn), who was known to be keen on a bonnie lass, Jessie Cowe. The lads clambered into the clock tower and after much hilarity and drinking of toasts the clock was named 'Jessie' in the young lady's honour. Jessie, a respected member of St Andrew's church choir, subsequently married a J. A. Cunningham and emigrated to Argentina. She must have returned home, however, for she is interred in Preston Kirk churchyard. 'Jessie's' centenary was celebrated in April 1988 with an exhibition and social gathering.

Parish schools

After the Reformation, responsibility for providing schooling fell to the Church. The first school was held in the church itself, in Bothwell's Aisle (perhaps where the Smeaton-Hepburn burial vault is today). The parish records of the seventeenth century contain numerous references to the need to remove the school from the church, with appeals to the heritors to carry this out. Eventually a site was found in Preston village a little to the east of the church, and this was the school which no doubt George and John Rennie attended, returning home via Andrew Meikle's workshop at Houston Mill, to which they were both drawn.

Another 'old boy' of the school at this date was Peter Nicholson, who won renown as a mathematician, architect and inventor. Born in the parish in 1765, he first helped his father, a local stone mason, before being apprenticed at the age of 12 to a cabinet maker in Linton. From there he progressed to a profession in architecture, and among his creations are Corby Castle, additions to the old Glasgow University and a town plan to establish Ardrossan as a watering-place. He opened schools for mechanics and in 1835 became President of the Newcastle Society for the promotion of the Fine Arts. He died in 1844.

In 1794, the parish school and schoolhouse were moved from Preston to a more central position in Linton (now Abbey House in Bridge Street). In the following year a weekly boarding school, or academy, for boys was opened by the Rev. Dr. Hugh Jamieson (see his portrait on page 64), minister of the U.P. Church, from his manse at the east end of Langside. Among the pupils there in 1826-7 was Charles Hay, son of William Hay of Lerwick, in Shetland! Clearly Dr. Jamieson's reputation as a schoolmaster had spread far from the parish, a fact attested on his tombstone in Preston Kirk graveyard, on which he is described both as 'a teacher of youth' and 'a successful teacher'. He died in 1863.

By the time the Rev. James Thomson wrote his account in 1835 there were five schools in the parish: 'parochial schools 2; one of which is a female school upheld by the heritors; private unendowed schools, 2, of which one is female; subscription school, 1'. The names of the parish schoolmaster, George Pringle Smith, and the schoolmistress of Linton Ladies' Boarding School, Miss Robertson, appear in the *Haddington Register and Almanac* for 1843.

In that same year, a Free Church school was added to the total. Housed initially in St. Andrew's Church, within two years its roll had risen to 140 pupils and a hall was built beside the church to hold them. The parish schools continued to serve the population until 1881 when all the masters and pupils transferred to a new State school built by the newly-appointed School Board. They also erected a nice new house for the schoolmaster at the west end of Langside (no.10 - and still inhabited by school teachers).

[30] East Linton Primary School, opened in 1881.

The Burgh of East Linton

In 1863, East Linton was formally declared a Burgh, thereby giving it greater control over its own affairs. John Porteous, a saddler and one of the town's leading tradesmen, was elected its first Chief Magistrate; the title was changed to Provost following the passing of the Burgh Police Act in 1892. The police station itself was at the north end of the High

Street (no.83), facing down Preston Road; the police cells are still in evidence. It was eventually replaced when the Town Council acquired Linton House, on Bridge Street (now Ark House) in 1949, and adapted it to provide two police houses, a charge room and a detention room.

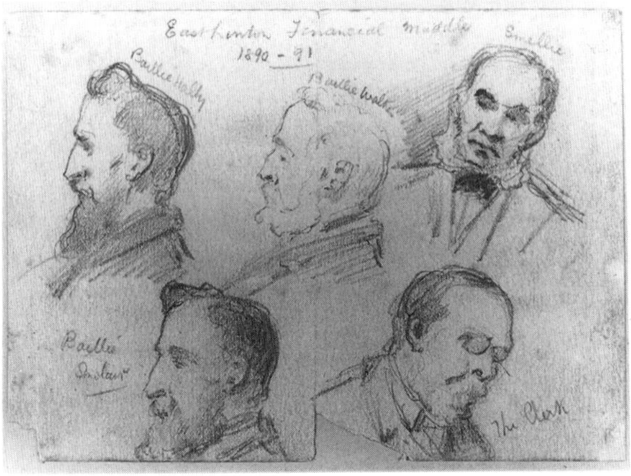

[31] A satirical pencil sketch by Arthur Melville of the burgh officials 1890-91.

In 1863 the population of the Burgh stood at 835, but it was set for a dramatic rise. By 1871 it had grown to 1037, an increase of 25%. The signs of that prodigious growth and prosperity are self-evident to this day. For example, many of the houses up Mill Wynd, around The Square and down the High Street show signs of having been heightened by a storey from their original single-storey form during the latter part of the nineteenth century. New housing developed along Brown's Place, School Road, Langside and Lauder Place. The Auction Mart, close beside the former railway station, was built about 1850 for hosting cattle sales. The Drill Hall (now the Community Hall) was erected in 1874 at a cost of £1000 for use by No 5 (East Linton) Company of the Haddington Rifle Volunteers, founded in 1860. It soon became a regular venue for lectures, concerts and exhibitions.

Other signs of prosperity included the building in the 1840s of a gasworks at the bottom of Lauder Place, operated by the East Linton

Gas Light Co. (it closed in the early 1960s). In the 1860s a branch of the National Bank of Scotland opened at no.8 High Street (now 'Old Bank House'; the present bank premises in Bank Road were opened on 3 May 1898). In 1881 a proper water-distribution and sewage system was installed. Cholera and other diseases had up till then been a constant source of concern, to which the inscriptions on some of the gravestones in the churchyard testify; hence the building of the cholera hospital, on Drylawhill Common, in 1832.

Garry S. Menzies

[32] A detail from the Fountain in The Square.

The new water-supply drew water from a spring in what is now Stories Park - the Peerie Well - which was pumped up to a tank near the Orchard. In the following year (1882) those waters were put to creative effect when the cast-iron Fountain was erected in The Square at the expense of John Drysdale, a Lintonian who had emigrated to Buenos Ayres and become a successful cattle trader. The Fountain was cast by George Smith & Co. at the Sun Foundry, Glasgow. Before the new water supply was introduced, Linton folk drew their water from a number of wells, including the old well on the site of the present Fountain, at Kingsburgh Gardens and the Peerie Well itself.

The piped water-supply was soon used to replace the primitive fire-fighting facilities, enabling standpipes and hose to be used. The horse-drawn fire-fighting vehicle that had to be called from Dunbar was also replaced from 1883 by the Burgh's own Fire Brigade so that it 'might rely upon having some responsible parties for the effectual appliance of hoses in future in the case of a fire occurring'. The Brigade initially consisted of six men who were paid £1 per year. In 1937 the Town Council provided a trailer pump drawn by a taxi, the latter supplied by the Firemaster, Fred Avery, who ran two of the town's garages. In 1939 responsibility for the volunteer members of the Auxiliary Fire Service passed to the National Fire Service. In 1961 the present Fire Station in Brown's Place was built to house a fire engine equipped with telescopic ladders and capable of carrying 400 gallons of water - still manned locally by 10 men.

In 1865 Prestonkirk House, at the junction of the High Street and Preston Road, was opened as the East Lothian Combination Poorhouse. It was built to serve 15 county parishes, including of course Prestonkirk. Dunbar made a bid to host the facility, but East Linton won the day because of 'its salubrity and convenience of access'. It had accommodation for 88 inmates, and its first Governor was William Merry.

There was unemployment too, and about 1875 the Rev. Thomas Marjoribanks, the Church of Scotland minister, had a block of houses built in School Road (nos.5-12) to create work in the parish. Rodger's Buildings at no.59 High Street was financed by the Rev. R. G. Rodger, the Free Church minister, about the same time.

So intense was all this building activity in the burgh that the *Haddingtonshire Courier*, in one of its numerous bulletins recording the pace of change dated 18 March 1881, reported that 'the topographic aspect of this thriving place is changing so rapidly that the oldest inhabitant will soon be out of his reckoning for its ancient landmarks'.

Beyond the burgh, the parish also thrived, and the signs of that prosperity are still there to be seen, with remodelled and extended farmhouses, impressive new steadings and farm workers' cottages being built. The steadings and cottages at Phantassie and Sunnyside both date from the 1850s, and the steading at Traprain from 1872.

Festival days

The East Linton Gala is familiar to most of us (see Chapter 8), but the event as we know it today was not the first of its kind to be celebrated within the parish. Auld Hansel Monday, Linton Race Day, Fastern's-e'en and a variety of events to commemorate royal coronations and jubilees have all merited places of importance in the social calendar over the years.

AULD HANSEL MONDAY

In the nineteenth century, before Christmas and New Year became established as festive days in Scotland, Auld Hansel Monday, the first Monday after 12 January, was the main break for rural folk in the long, hard days of winter; and moreover the schools were also closed on the Tuesday! It took its name from the simple giving of the hand in friendship, troth or bargain-making, and the Anglo-Saxon words *hand* (hand) and *sellen* (to give) give a reasonable clue to the origin.

Auld Hansel Monday was a more important day to Linton folks than New Year's Day. Farm work was suspended for the day and many people used the occasion to visit friends. For those who decided to remain in Linton a suitable field was 'commissioned' for the Hansel Monday games which included athletics and football competitions and attracted many professional 'peds' from all over the county. The final games, just before the end of the century, were held in the Toll Field, to the east of Lauder Place, on the Phantassie Estate. They were almost a wash-out since snow had fallen and was in the process of melting when the games commenced.

The Hansel Monday Ball or Dance was the outstanding night of the year. It was looked forward to with great anticipation - by the lassies especially! It would last well into the following morning, with the happy gathering of old and young dancing to the music of the local band.

CARTERS' PLAY DAY or LINTON RACE DAY

The East Linton Carters' Friendly Society was formed in 1824 and disbanded about 1865. The carters and their drays were used for a variety of jobs, but mainly for the transit of produce from the local distillery to Dunbar, whence it was shipped to London.

The great event in the year was the Carters' Play, otherwise known as Linton Race Day, when the carters, many dressed in sleeved waistcoats and 'bo-yanks', turned out with their horses and carts beautifully decorated with ribbons, brasses, bells and flowers. A procession, headed by 'Mi' Lord' and his 'Left and Right-Hand Bailies' and accompanied by the local instrumental band, toured the town and stopped off at various nominated 'watering holes' along the route.

These places of attraction included the mansion houses on the Smeaton and Phantassie estates. Geordie Hunter, whose premises were at the bottom of the High Street near Tyne Road, was the last person to officiate as 'Mi' Lord', and the last two Bailies were James Campbell and Alexander Clapperton.

The carters rode the marches, or boundaries, of the parish before commencing the races that were held in the field opposite Phantassie Square. Cart horses, van horses, and even 'cuddies' at times, competed. Many travelling showmen visited, and stalls were erected in the street where a variety of novelties and commodities were displayed and sold. The most popular was the stall where gingerbread, in the shape of men, horses or cows, could be bought; gingerbread was evidently considered a special treat in those days.

The Carters' Flag, presented to them at their inception in 1824 by Lady Mary Buchan-Hepburn, still exists and is kept in the Council Chamber at no.30 High Street. The front bears the inscription: 'The Carters' Friendly Society of East Linton - established July 31st 1824'. It also depicts the square and compasses above two carters shaking hands. A horse drawing a cart loaded with three casks is also featured. It is interesting to note that each of the barrels bears the stamp '25 o.p.', believed to refer to the potency of the liquor. The reverse carries the quotation: 'Behold how good and how pleasant it is for brethren to dwell together in unity', and bears a representation of two trotting horses and two horses in yoke. The flag was supported on two rose-crowned standards and proudly carried by the two Bailies in the Society's annual parade.

John W. Steele

[33] One side of the Carters' Flag.

FASTERN'S-E'EN

The traditional marking of the winter's end, and the using up of the household's rich foodstuffs before the austere fasting of Lent, has been celebrated since pagan times on the eve of Ash Wednesday. It was also known as Fasten's-e'en, Mardis Gras and Shrove (Pancake) Tuesday.

On Fasten-e'en we had a rockin',
To ca' the crack and weave our stockin';
And there was muckle fun and jokin'
Ye need na doubt;
At length we had a hearty yokin',
At 'sang about'.
(Robert Burns *Epistle to J. Lapraik*, 1785)

In East Linton, Fastern's-e'en was the occasion for a game of 'football' between the married and single men; the ball was made by the local shoemaker. Adam Craies, whose business was at no.13 High Street, had the honour of making the ball for the final match in 1886. The ball was filled with hay seed and decorated with ribbons, and the game was kicked off from the Old Well (where the Fountain now stands) by the most recently married man in the town. The 'field' was the High Street. The goal for the married men was the Tyne at Prestonkirk House, for the single men the far side of Linton Bridge. After a tough struggle between many more than the regulation 11 players on each side, the 'match' usually ended up in a pond that the youngsters formed by damming the Easy Burn. This ran along Brown's Place and turned at the bottom of the High Street to join the Tyne just below where Stories Park is now. It was customary to have a pail or two full of whisky from the town distillery placed at the side of the pond to revive the exhausted participants!

DUMPLIN' DAY

Dumplin' Day, also held in February, was when the town bakers sold large dumplings filled with fruit. These were specially made for the day and Linton folk deemed them a tremendous treat.

Private Collection

[34] Robert Noble's The Artist's Garden. *This was his last canvas, painted in the garden of his house at no.2 Preston Road.*

Chapter 7

EAST LINTON ARTISTS

An artist's paradise

East Linton has a long tradition of landscape painting. From the late 1880s artists were attracted from all over Scotland and from England also. The picturesque Burgh offered many appealing aspects. The River Tyne especially, flowing slowly between tall sprawling willows, and then surging through the Linn jaws, past ancient mills, colourful orchards and golden fields, provided painting subjects for which there was a ready market. The railway station ensured easy access for the visiting artists, and bills for seasonal lodgings could be settled with paint on canvas. Little wonder that by 1906 East Linton had become known as 'The Scottish Barbizon', comparing it to the French village in the Forest of Fontainebleau, which had become the resort of realist painters from the 1840s onwards. However, before the main influx of painters, three prominent artists had spent their childhood in East Linton - Pettie, Hardie and Melville.

Pettie, Hardie and Melville

JOHN PETTIE (1839-93)

John Pettie's parents, Alexander and Alison Pettie, bought a grocery at no.9 The Square in 1852 when John was aged 13. There is a local story that when John was sent on an errand to the storeroom of his father's shop he would draw on the lid of a bow or a cask and completely forget the errand. Using the house painting material in the store he

[35] A portrait of John Pettie.

painted at the age of 15 a picture of the village carrier and his donkey. The local verdict was recorded: 'If it isna Jock Little and his cuddy; its sae life-like its no canny'.

This exceptional talent enabled Pettie to enrol at the Trustees' Academy in Edinburgh in 1855. He frequently returned to East Linton, together with other students and friends, including William McTaggart. Later he moved to London and gained fame as a painter of historical subjects.

CHARLES MARTIN HARDIE (1858-1916)

Charles Martin Hardie, a relation of Pettie's, was born in Brown's Place, East Linton, where his family had a joinery business. The business then moved to Bridge End Villa (where McArthur's is today) and was managed for some years by Charles's mother after his father's death in 1870. Encouraged by John Pettie, the young Hardie developed his talent for drawing. Original leanings towards architecture were overtaken by a flair for sketching and painting.

Ambition caused Hardie to leave East Linton at the age of 17, to enroll at the Edinburgh School of Design. From there he proceeded to the Life School of the Royal Scottish Academy. He became a prominent painter of historical scenes and book illustrator, and lived the later part of his life at North Queensferry. Following his death in 1916 his body was interred in Preston Kirk churchyard.

ARTHUR MELVILLE (1855-1904)

Arthur Melville was born in Angus, but came to East Linton as a small child when his father took up a position as a coachman on the Smeaton Estate. Young Arthur, after attending the village school, served his apprenticeship with a grocer in the High Street, almost opposite the competing shop run by the Pettie family. Bored with retailing, Melville moved first to Dalkeith and then to Edinburgh where he became a student of the RSA Schools. He was taught by J. Campbell Noble. He quickly developed into one of Scotland's most celebrated watercolour artists. He travelled widely, especially in North Africa, the Middle East and Spain, before dying of typhoid at the early age of 49. His sketch of the burgh officials in 1890-1 is reproduced on page 78.

A hub of pastoral art

These three local artists - Pettie, Hardie and Melville - no doubt drew the attention of their fellow students in Edinburgh to the painting possibilities in the East Linton area. Meanwhile, landscape painting had been gathering pace elsewhere in East Lothian. Ever since the time of Turner's visits, the East Lothian coastline, especially the dramatic views of Tantallon Castle and the Bass Rock, had attracted many well-known artists. Perhaps more significantly, by 1870 William Darling McKay (1844-1924) was painting in the Gifford area scenes of country-folk at work. He was painting in a manner not dissimilar to that of the earlier French realists. McKay's example was followed by others, particularly Robert McGregor, who portrayed the hard graft of farm labour before the days of mechanisation in an unsentimental down-to-earth manner. By the late 1880s East Linton had become a hub of pastoral art in East Lothian.

Robert Noble (1857-1917)

Around 1885 a young landscape and figure artist by the name of Robert Noble was visiting East Linton and realising the possibilities of the locality. Perhaps it was no coincidence that Robert Noble was a fellow student and close friend of Charles Martin Hardie. For a while they shared a studio in Picardy Place, Edinburgh. In 1887, Noble settled in East Linton where he was to live for the remaining 30 years of his life. He became the central figure of the local artistic fraternity.

Robert Noble originated from the east end of Edinburgh. His father, Thomas, and his father's brother, James, had both been blacksmiths at Lyne in Peeblesshire, in the rural Tweed valley, but moved to Abbeyhill to labour on the rapidly-expanding railway network, and later in St. Margaret's railway engineering workshops at Meadowbank. The families of the two brothers grew up in neighbouring tenements in Abbeyhill.

When Robert Noble was born in 1857, his neighbour and cousin, James Campbell Noble, was then aged 10. Campbell Noble, as

Roger Durman

[36] Robert Noble at work

he became known, trained as an engineering draughtsman, then as a lithographer and finally as an artist. It was Campbell Noble who taught his young cousin the skills of lithography and art. After serving an apprenticeship as a lithographer, Robert entered the Trustees' School in Edinburgh where he excelled. His training continued at an atelier in Paris during successive winters in the early 1880s. Summers were spent with other artists either in Grez, to the south of Paris, or at Buckhaven in Fife. At Buckhaven Noble painted fisherfolk beside the quaint old buildings of the harbour town. Here he met Christian Balfour Greig, a local draper's daughter, whom he married in 1876.

By this time Noble was also visiting East Linton. The following spring he and his young wife opted to settle here. The couple lodged first at Drylawhill Farm before moving to the town centre and eventually to a new house in Preston Road (no.2; 'The Neuk'). From the outset it was the River Tyne flowing through Prestonkirk parish which attracted Noble's growing talent - the flow past the foot of the steep sided orchard, the flow beneath the old stone bridge, the flow through the mill lade, past the sluices, beside the town mills and the cascade through the linn and into the deep pool beneath, past Houston Mill and Preston Kirk and past the haugh meadow with picturesque Preston Mill capped by its quaint roofs of red pantiles. Down stream the river banks and mill lade, clad with tall grey-green willows, extending to Knowes Mill and beyond, provided potential for so many colourful canvases, large and small.

From 1888 onwards paintings by Robert Noble from scenes along this two-mile stretch of river were exhibited prominently in Edinburgh, London and beyond. Paintings such as "Preston Mill", "The River Sluice", "After the Spate" and many more were admired at the Edinburgh RSA exhibitions of the time, while others such as "The Linn Jaws" and "By the Linn Pool" were shown at the Royal Academy in London. By 1890 the fame of both Robert Noble and the East Linton Tyne was spreading through the capitals.

An influx of artists

The growing reputation of East Linton as a fashionable place to paint attracted many artists. Few were long-term residents; some came for the summer season or for shorter stays and some visited for a day, travelling by train from Edinburgh. One of the first residents after Robert Noble's arrival was Thomas Bromley Blacklock, who often chose woodland scenes. In 1892 he illustrated "Sketches in East Lothian" with 32 fine drawings. Later he moved to Kirkcudbright where his now well-known paintings of woodland incorporated children and fairy-tale scenes.

Private Collection

[37] Thomas Bromley Blacklock's sketch of Hailes Castle and the River Tyne from his "Sketches in East Lothian". James Purves, in his introduction to the "Sketches", wrote of the castle that it "...nestles cosily beneath the shadow of Traprain, beside the murmering Tyne."

Another permanent resident of East Linton was William Ferguson, a colourful character who lived for 17 years in a caravan near Knowes Mill before his death in 1922. With his violin he enlivened many evening gatherings in The Crown or Red Lion hotels. He also shared Robert Noble's enthusiasm for local sport, especially golf and curling.

Various writings from the early Edwardian years describe the artists at work along the River Tyne. A magazine article in 1906 recorded how seven or eight easels could be seen at one time set up on the riverside below the linn. Two years later a biography of John Pettie referred to the same stretch of the Tyne, comparing the number of artists at work with those at the foreshore of Newlyn or St Ives, where at times one had to walk with caution for fear of tripping over a leg of an easel or setting a foot in a box of oily tubes.

In spite of this concentration on landscape painting, a definable East Linton 'school' did not develop. Whilst the river, with its mills and willows, became the central theme of so many pictures, painting styles remained individual and varied.

Only a handful of visiting artists can be mentioned individually. William Miller Frazer, who originated from Perth, was a great friend of Noble and a frequent visitor to East Linton. His subtle oils of pastoral scenes were painted in a flowing impressionist style. During his remarkably long artistic career he exhibited for 71 consecutive years, before dying at the ripe old age of 96. Robert Hope, who was principally a society portrait painter in Edinburgh, frequently visited East Linton for a month or two in summer to paint simple rustic scenes. James Whitelaw Hamilton, who was associated with 'The Glasgow Boys', painted in East Linton around 1907-1915. Of the same celebrated group, James Paterson produced beautiful watercolours of the river and woods in Prestonkirk parish.

Farm animals in the meadows became the favourite subjects of a few specialists. Joseph Farquharson, later famed for his scenes of sheep in snow, had trained with Robert Noble in the same Paris studio. Before returning to his family's Aberdeenshire estate, Farquharson had worked around East Linton. John Gauld, who produced so many restful pictures of calves, was also a well-known visitor. Andrew Douglas, perhaps best known for his pictures of cattle in Highland settings, painted at the farms in Prestonkirk for many years.

Following Robert Noble's death in 1917 there was a slow decline in the number of visiting artists, but the magnetism of the area never died, still drawing artists of the Noble era. Today, many amateur artists, and the occasional professional, may be seen at work around Preston Mill. The tradition lives on with an annual exhibition in East Linton of their work, started in 1968 by the Traders' Association and now run by the East Linton and District Community Association.

The Grey Road - Prestonkirk Obituary to Robert Noble

[38] The bronze image of Robert Noble from his headstone in Preston Kirk churchyard.

For 30 years, Robert Noble lived in East Linton, and 30 years he found were too short to exhaust the beauties it held for his brush. Every year he gave us fresh and joyous transcriptions of the scenes between Hailes and the Knowes. The quiet reaches of the Tyne above the village, the rush and tumble of the water through the Linn jaws, the smooth flow past the willows down towards the church pool, the mill in the meadow, the green sward with cattle grazing, the guardian trees around St Baldred's Well, the 'siller saughs' that shroud the still waters, the far-stretching distances - all these yielded him worthy subjects, and by his loving labours he made East Linton famous beyond his native land.

We have often gone down that road together - the grey road that winds above the banks of the river, between his home and the old church. We would look over the moss-grown wall, and see the trout lying in the pool, or watch the coot and water-hen scurrying across the quiet reflections of the trees in the stream. We would climb the path that turned through the little hillocks of green grass, beside the shadowed side of the church, and look down on the river, seen in silver breaks through the leafy screen. He would say there was no more beautiful spot on earth than this - no more restful place.

And today, he and I, with many more, are wending down the grey road to the green hill by the church. But there seems to be a veil between the sun and the earth, a mist coming up the valley from the sea. There are many more shadows on the road, which seems steeper than yesterday. The willows whiten and shiver down in the valley - there is a stillness over the trees, though somewhere the birds are singing. Why are they singing?

We are going down the road today - but he is strangely silent. Yet I know he is with us through this vibrant air. The tread of the bearers' feet is muffled as we wend on through God's little acre of green, past the old church tower, to the other side where the sun is shining on the dear brown earth - dearer now for what it receives in trust.

Once again we are alone on the grey road - and only the birds are singing.

W. M. Frazer, ARSA
from the Haddingtonshire Courier,
25 May 1917

Chapter 8

CLUBS AND SOCIETIES

Something for everyone

Clubs and societies have formed a major part in the social life of East Linton over many years. A variety were formed in Victorian and Edwardian times, but only a few of them survive today. These are the Horticultural Society (founded 1859), Masonic Lodge Tyneside 714 (1885), some of the sports clubs - Curling (1838), Bowling (1863), Football (1878) and Golf (1897) - and the Scout Troop (1908).

The rest are all long defunct. They included a number of Friendly Societies, like the Ancient Order of Foresters - Court 'Hope of Lothian (1878), a Choral Union and a Total Abstinence Society (both 1882), a Literary Society (1886), a Burns (and Scott) Club (1896), a Quoiting Club (1897), an Ornithological Society and Good Templars' Lodge 'Star of the Linn' (both 1898). There was even a Combination Hearse Society, formed in 1865 in an attempt to reduce the cost of hiring the hearse for funerals!

During this century the Young Men's Mutual Improvement Association, Young Men's Christian Association, Young Women's Christian Association, Comrades of the Great War, Draughts Club, Putting Club, 'Keep Fit' Club, Ladies' Whist Club, Swimming Club, Tenants' Association, Traders' Association, Cycling Club and Motorcycle Club, among several others, have all come and gone.

The Cricket Club perhaps has the distinction of being the shortest-lived. It was formed around 1900 by a group of youths who had been collecting money for a football. When a certain gentleman, who had no interest in football, offered them 10 shillings if they formed a cricket club instead, they readily accepted and hastily founded one. Since there was no pitch, the club used the school playground on Saturday mornings. Unfortunately, and perhaps predictably, only a few

Saturdays after the club's foundation a speeding ball shattered one of the classroom windows. The Police arrived and confiscated the equipment, which was never seen again.

Music and drama

In days gone by, East Linton had its artistic moments. In Victorian times there was both a Flute Band and a Brass Band. They co-existed for a time, although not always harmoniously. So great was the rivalry between them in fact that on occasions members came to 'unmusical' blows. Eventually a truce was signed and they amalgamated in 1886 when 14 people volunteered their services to form an Instrumental Band. The conductor was Hugh Ross who played both the cornet and the violin. Despite financial problems, the band survived into the early 1900s, performing with great skill at most local celebrations.

In the first half of this century there was a very good dramatic club, producing such plays as *Rob Roy*, *Jeannie Deans* and *All that Glitters is not Gold*. There were several leading lights in the company but undoubtedly the most notable was the local tailor, P. T. Anderson.

Prestonkirk Women's Rural Institute (established in 1920) contributed much to local entertainment and in the 1930s and '40s their Mixed Voice Choir staged several concerts in the Drill Hall. During the '40s and '50s the W.R.I. Dramatic Club produced plays like *Jennie*, *Guests at Glentaggart* and *Quiet Weekend*, and at North Berwick in 1953 won the Scottish Community Drama Association's Croal Trophy with *Among Those Present*. The stage manager at that triumph was a certain Jim Menzies, who is today the Chairman of the East Linton Local History Society. The Club then took the production to the Divisional Final Festival in Falkirk.

East Linton's musical tradition continued into the 1960s when members of the local Youth Club formed a 'pop' group, 'the Lintones'! The original members played their first 'live' performance at a social event in the Drill Hall in November 1963. The arrival of Bobby McIntyre from Dunbar in December saw the band change its name first to 'The Lynn Rockers with Bobby' and then to 'Bobby & the Kaskades', and their popularity spread far beyond East Linton. With Bobby's departure in the mid-'60s, the group, by now re-named 'Nature's Things', went into decline.

Horticultural Society

The Horticultural Society is one of the oldest in Scotland and held its first Show on Monday 31 October 1859 in Smellie's Hall in the Red Raw. One of the most unusual prizes, for the best grapes grown in the open air, was won by Mr. G. Finlayson. Entrants had to declare whether they were 'amateurs' or 'cottagers'; an amateur was one who 'employed skilled assistance' whereas a cottager was one who raised his produce 'with no assistance beyond that of his family or unskilled labour'. Annual spring and autumn shows were held during the early years, but these eventually gave way to the now firmly-established August Show.

Curling Club

The Curling Club was formed in 1838, and was one of the original members of the Grand Caledonian Curling Club, which became the Royal Caledonian Curling Club (R.C.C.C.) in 1842. East Linton continued its membership of the R.C.C.C. until 1952 and rejoined in 1968 when the Club was reconstituted.

The 21 founder members of the Club played on Lawhead Pond by kind permission of Andrew Howden. Around the mid-1850s, Smeaton Lake became the preferred meeting-place when Sir Thomas Buchan-Hepburn made the venue available to the rapidly expanding membership. In 1860, the Club enjoyed success when the Lord Elcho Cup was won for the first time. This feat was repeated in 1914 (when the cup was proudly displayed in Provost Barrie's grocery shop window in The Square for a few days), and in successive years 1977 and 1978, with John Smith, farmer in Cairndinnis, as skip on both occasions.

A second Curling Club - Tyneside - was formed in 1910 and played on the artificial pond on the site of the old bowling green off

George Laing

[39] Curling on Smeaton Lake in Victorian times.

Lauder Place. Robert Noble was instrumental in establishing this Club and was its secretary from its inception until his death in 1917. The two clubs continued to co-exist until 1931 when they amalgamated to become the East Linton Curling Club, once again with Sir John Buchan-Hepburn as president. The members continued to play outdoors, mainly at Lauder Place, but occasionally on Smeaton Lake. As winters became less severe towards the late 1940s, so the Club moved indoors, to Haymarket Ice Rink, Edinburgh. Today, the Club plays at Murrayfield Ice Rink, also in Edinburgh. Recent successes have included the East Lothian Province Bonspiel in 1995 and 1996, and the East Lothian Province Royal Bank of Scotland Quaich in 1995.

The great outdoors is not totally ignored, however, and opportunities are seized whenever they present themselves. In March 1947, a full week's play was held on the Tyne and the sharp frosts of January 1982 allowed some people to sample the delights of 'the roaring game' on Smeaton Lake for the first time.

Bowling Club

East Linton Bowling Club was formed in 1862 and after a number of years at Lauder Place moved to its present green on Bank Road, which was opened by A. J. Balfour, M.P., of Whittingehame House, on 18 September 1880. In order to provide better amenities for the members, a small clubhouse was erected in 1884.

The green was purchased from the Trustees of Phantassie Estate in 1919 for £170, electricity was installed in 1930, the green radically altered in 1952, and a new clubhouse extension opened by Provost D. M. Rennie in 1974. Artificial banks and an automatic watering system were installed in 1983 and a further extension added to the clubhouse in 1990.

John W. Steele

[40] The S.B.A. 'Fours' champions of 1979 with the McEwan Trophy.
Ian Butler, John Scott, Heb Milligan, David Currie

The Club joined the Scottish Bowling Association (S.B.A.) in 1893 and in the same year qualified for the finals of the Scottish Fours Championship at Queen's Park, Glasgow - the first year of that competition. Since then, several players have reached the S.B.A. finals, and of those pride of place must be reserved for David Currie, Ian Butler, John Scott and Heb Milligan who won the 'Fours' in 1979 and then went on to capture the British Isles Fours title at Nottingham the following year. East Linton's 'bard', Hugh Munro, captured the magic of the Scottish Championship win in a celebratory poem, the first verse of which ran:

Twas August Fourth, a date tae mark,
A' Linton's thoughts were at Queen's Park,
Where on that famous Boolin' Green,
Bathed in a brilliant summer scene,
Four Linton lads went oot that day,
A' Scotland marvelled at their play,
And though the best they had tae meet,
I'm proud tae say, they wer'na beat.

At County level, the Club has enjoyed success over a long period. It was the first winner of the East Lothian Bowling Association's Jubilee Cup in 1887, a feat repeated 19 times since, the most recent being in 1996, and has won the County Cup also on 20 occasions. International selection has so far eluded the men, but Mrs. Janet Milligan, a prominent member of the Ladies' Section (formed in 1973), was selected to represent Scotland in the Home International Series in Edinburgh in 1985, and again in Wales the following year.

Football Clubs

In 1878 an Athletic Society was formed in East Linton after a field (the Manse Field, now the Glebe) was made available for a recreation ground by Sir David Baird and the Rev. T. S. Marjoribanks. A football club was immediately formed and the first game was played on the ground on 16 November that same year.

The first East Linton team performed admirably to reach the last eight of the Edinburgh Shield (East of Scotland Shield) in season 1883-4. Unfortunately they were drawn against the then mighty Hibernian Football Club and played at Easter Road on 18 December. After losing eight goals in the first half, the team returned home with a 10-0 drubbing. It is interesting to note that Hibs did go on to win the trophy, scoring 30 goals and conceding only 2 in the entire competition. On 16 January 1886, in the final of the Edinburgh Association Consolation Cup, East Linton lost 0-7 to the Adventurers (Edinburgh) at Tynecastle Park. Easter Road proved not to be a happy hunting ground for our local team. They returned there in 1887, again in the Edinburgh Shield, this time losing 0-9 to another Edinburgh team, Norton Park. Three trips to Edinburgh - 0 goals for, 26 against!

The Club was a member of the Haddingtonshire Football Association, and won the Association Cup in 1885. Since there were insufficient funds for medals that year, the team decided to retain the Cup, much to the annoyance of some Haddington lads who decided to retrieve the trophy; but in a physical 'confrontation' at Pencraig the Linton lads recaptured the prize. After its return, a 'guardian' decided that the Cup would be out of danger in the safe-keeping of the Tyne, so he attached an old kettle to the trophy and threw it into the river. Later, a young girl is believed to have fished it out, but the Cup was never seen again.

So popular was the game becoming that other football clubs were formed in the burgh; these included East Linton Harp (1896), East Linton St Clair (1898), East Linton Wednesday (1908), East Linton United (1912), East Linton Corinthians (1930), East Linton Tyne Vale (1938), East Linton Youth Club (1940s) and East Linton Thistle (1960s).

St Clair were founder members of the East Lothian Juvenile (Haldane) League in 1901 and won both the League title and the Angus Cup in the 1904-5 season. St Clair F.C.'s success was continued by another juvenile team, East Linton United, who won the Dalrymple Cup in season 1913-14. The Corinthians brought the Angus Cup back to East Linton in 1934.

Perhaps the most successful, and best known, of the local football teams was East Linton Tyne Vale. Their most memorable season was 1951-2 when they entered four different cup competitions - the Scottish Amateur, East of Scotland, Logan and Hamilton Cups. They reached the fourth round of the Scottish, and the final of the other three competitions, winning the Logan and Hamilton Cups, and being beaten by the odd goal in three by Dalkeith Thistle in the East of Scotland trophy.

John W. Steele

[41] East Linton Tyne Vale FC, in 1952
J. Bald, T. Watson, A. Lamb, P. Kerr, D. Skinner, R. Crail, D. Rutherford, W. Craig, W. Hunter, R. Purves, G. Reid, R. Craik, T. Skinner, W. Black, F. Yeats and K. Fletcher (mascot)

Today, the local amateur team, East Linton Thistle, continues the proud tradition of football in East Linton. One of their best seasons to date was 1981-2 when they won both the Angus Cup and the Eastern League Championship.

Golf Club

'The club wi' nae hame' is an apt description for East Linton Golf Club since, despite celebrating its centenary in 1997, it has never had a golf course to call its own!

The first record of the Club is contained in a minute of a meeting, called by Robert Noble, the artist, and held in Dakers' Coffee

House, in School Road (now Abbeyfield), on 21 January 1897. Although just nine gentlemen attended the meeting, Noble had earlier secured the promises of another 23 potential members, and so the Club was formed and Noble became its first captain.

The initial idea was to set out a nine-hole course in the school park, but this was soon abandoned in favour of one on the Longstone field on Pencraig, the property of Mr. Lee, the farmer at Markle. The Rev. T. S. Marjoribanks presented the Club with a lawnmower for use on the putting greens. The first competition on this nine-hole course, 'Captain Noble's Monthly Handicap Medal', was played on 20 and 23 October 1897. Mr. Short of Whittingehame saw off the other 21 competitors with a scratch score of 104!

Sandy Watt

[42] Members of the golf club outside Gifford clubhouse about 1910.
W. Watt, ?, A. Davidson,
T.Black, R. Dalgleish, A. Walker, ?, ? Bryson.

In the following year, the Club moved to the 'Common' ground offered by Mr. Bell of East Fortune who retained the right of grazing over the course. The first competition there was held on 7 December, but darkness set in and stopped play; no scores were returned!

For reasons unknown, the original Golf Club was soon disbanded and a new one, with membership limited to 40, was constituted at a meeting in Smellie's Hall on 11 February 1902. This coincided with Mr. St Clair Cunningham offering the use of his golf course at Hedderwickhill. The inaugural match there was played on 26 March, and in the following month club badges were issued at 9d each. In that same year, the Club was also presented with a gold medal by John Lumsden, the local headmaster, in memory of his school-teacher son, Oswald, and the first winner was A. Moncrieff, after a 4-man play-off. The Oswald Lumsden Gold Medal is still competed for annually by the members.

On 10 January 1925, farmer John Gifford holed the second at Hedderwickhill in one stroke, and in September 1926, Pat Butler, an excellent golfer, established a course record of 69. The Club continued to play there until 1937. Over the next few years, the 'nomads' competed enthusiastically over many courses throughout the County. Dunbar East Links became a favoured venue and since 1975 has been the Club's permanent 'home'. Nowadays, though, members of East Linton Golf Club must first become members of the Dunbar club.

Scouts and Guides

Scouting in East Linton dates back to 1908 when the first Troop (two patrols) was formed; it was among the first established in the country. All the boys later joined the 8th Battalion the Royal Scots and served in France during the Great War. A Cub Pack was formed in 1919 and a Rover Crew in 1935.

In 1929 the local troop won the County Troop Flag. In 1931, a change was made in the Troop Colours from yellow with a red border, which 'ran' rather badly with washing, to grey and red. The Scouts won the County Patrol Cup in 1936, the County Signalling Cup in 1954, and two years later the County Flag for the first time. The Wingate Cup, awarded to the best organised working Scout Group in East Lothian, was won for the only time in 1950. The County Flag returned to the Burgh in 1970. The Cubs, too, have had their successes, winning the County Flag in 1957, and the Blue Circle Shield (in the East Lothian Council's environmental competition) in 1994.

The story of Guiding in the parish dates back to 1923, when 25 girls enrolled as Guide recruits and two as Brownies at a gathering in the granary at Phantassie. The Prestonkirk Girl Guide Company was formally registered on 14 February 1924, and later that year they held their first camp at Pease Glen. In the same year the Misses Grant-Suttie took over as Captain and Lieutenant and continued in that capacity for 17 years, when Miss Hilda resigned and Miss Ethel became Captain; Miss Ethel resigned only in December 1945, after 21 years of distinguished service. The Company's Union Jack, presented by the Misses Grant-Suttie in 1924, is still carried today.

Among the highlights in the Company's history was the winning of the County Flag (donated incidentally by Miss Buchan-Hepburn) in 1929 and 1930. Lady Baden-Powell presented the former at a ceremony in Edinburgh's Usher Hall.

Jim Menzies

[43] The East Linton Scout Group with the Wingate Cup, 1950.

John W. Steele

[44] The burgh of East Linton viewed from Drylawhill at the beginning of the twentieth century.

Chapter 9

THE TWENTIETH CENTURY: WAR AND PEACE

Conservation and change

Despite the title of this section the older part of East Linton preserves an old-world appearance which suggests that it has not changed much over the last 200 years. In The Square and High Street the irregular line of buildings, old architectural forms and red-tiled roofs enhance that impression. The long association with so many artists and their work has developed in the people an appreciation of the place and some caution about removing the features in the interests of so-called progress.

The century has, however, brought far-reaching changes to conditions of life in East Linton and the parish of Prestonkirk. Early in the century the advent of the internal combustion engine, in motors cars and buses, began to improve the links within the parish and with other centres beyond. The wars brought many people into the district from other parts and took away many young men and women for long periods. This meant much more inter-marriage with people of other districts, and a number of ex-service men bringing their wives into the parish. All this had a subtle influence on the life, customs and outlook of the community.

The chief changes, however, came through the altered status of the farmer and farm-worker. Work on the land, though heavy, often dirty and lasting long hours, was poorly paid with basic remuneration in kind. Conditions of life were often primitive and rough, with few amenities. Only hard work, high principles and mutual affection in the family circle made homes the nurseries of ambition for success in life.

At the beginning of the century ploughing was done by the 'swing plough' which had no wheels and depended on the skill of the ploughman in setting his 'irons' (the sock and the coulter), on his eyesight and on his good workmanship. The ploughman fed his horses and cleaned the stalls and horses at 5am, ready for starting at 6am. There was a break for breakfast at 8am and a stop for dinner at 11am. The afternoon yoke was from 1pm to 6pm with no break. Then he had to feed, clean and bed his horses after they reached the stable. This went on six days a week; on Sunday there was morning and evening attendance at church.

The women workers also spent from 6am to 6pm in summer in the fields, the same hours as the men, but often with dirtier work and very poorly paid. Between 9 and 10 shillings per week was the common wage, and half of that for a 'halfin' who had newly left school at 11 or 12 years of age. Market-garden work (there were three around East Linton - at Houston Mill, Kingsburgh and the Orchard, beyond the by-pass) was done mostly by women and girls who wore head-dresses known as 'uglies' to protect them from the sun and wind. Much of the work was really back-breaking.

John W. Steele

[45] Stacking at Drylawhill c.1920
?, J. Kelly,
Jess McKinley, J. Christie, Mrs. Milligan, W. Milligan

The scythe and hook were disappearing from general harvest work and giving way to the reaper, and later the self-binder pulled at first by horses. The self-binder helped to reduce the work involved in building the stooks that were formed in the fields before being led in to form rows of tall stacks of grain. As the century advanced the tractor came more into use, and whereas there had been four, five or even six pairs of horses, they became reduced until there were none. The self-binder was in time replaced by the combine harvester and the stooks were no longer part of the harvest scene, being replaced at first by stacks. The number of farm workers as a result reduced greatly and the women and girls employed on the farms and market gardens found employment in the nearby towns.

The changes brought about by mechanisation improved in many respects the working and living conditions, status and wages of the farm worker. They may have become more isolated while at work, but they were now able to travel to their entertainment, so replacing the simpler home-grown amusements of the past.

East Linton in the Great War

The First and Second World Wars had a profound effect on the parish, and the War Memorial in the town's park bears the names of 38 men from the former and 14 from the latter who left the parish but did not return.

The Great War saw the calling to the colours of large numbers of young men in the parish. The Drill Hall was requisitioned by the military early in the war for training recruits. Smellie's Hall, in the Red Raw (Bridge Street), at that time the meeting place for Lodge Tyneside 714, became a hospital for a while, and the 'targets' across the Tyne from the Orchard to the south of the town were used for rifle practice. Army units stationed in and around East Linton included the 10th Royal Scots (Cyclists), and the Cameronians who were encamped at Phantassie. The East Linton platoon of 'B' Company 5th Volunteer Battalion, Royal Scots, was raised in October 1916. This was part of the force originally known as the East Lothian Volunteers.

George Laing

[46] The Royal Scots in front of the Drill Hall in 1914.

Mrs. Mina Craig

[47] Women at work at East Fortune airfield in World War One.

The women-folk helped in the task of sewing the material that formed the skins of the airships based at nearby East Fortune airfield. The airships were used for coastal patrols.

The minutes of the Burgh Council reveal concern with matters such as preserving water, fund-raising on flag days and the condition of the latrines at the Drill Hall! At the end of the war a letter of appreciation was received from Major Baird, commanding the troops locally, recording his thanks for the assistance of the burgh officials and the hospitality of the people.

Between the wars

The Armistice declared at 11am on 11 November 1918 saw the parish return to something approaching normality. Those serving in the forces fortunate enough to survive the horrors of the trenches came home to pick up the threads of their lives once more, whether on the farms and market gardens, or in the shops and businesses of the burgh. The Memorial Park in front of the school was thus named in 1920 in honour of those from the parish who had made the ultimate sacrifice.

The 1920s in particular saw considerable progress. At the beginning of the decade, the telephone made its appearance in the burgh, as the low telephone numbers of the businesses noted on page 111 testify to. (The kiosk in front of no.23 High Street is so fine an example of the K6-type designed in 1935 by Giles Gilbert Scott that it has recently been listed by Historic Scotland as a category B listed building.) 1928 saw the opening of the by-pass road, with two modern bridges to carry the road over river and railway; the inadequacy of Linton Bridge to carry the increasing traffic had been evident for some time. In the following year electricity arrived in the town, and the two churches in the parish - Preston Kirk and St Andrew's - reunited (the Free Church and the U.P. Church had previously united in 1910). So there came to be two congregations of the Church of Scotland in the parish which were eventually united under one minister in 1959. (A Catholic chapel, St Kentigern's - now Nonesuch House - had opened in the High Street in 1913.)

Roger Durman

[48] An old postcard view of the top end of the High Street between the wars.

Most of the shops and businesses in East Linton served the farming community in some way. Blacksmiths and joiners made and repaired most of the farm implements, and their premises were often placed close to each other so that they could co-operate when making or 'ringing' cartwheels. Saddlers produced the harness, collars and saddlery. A peep into Mr. Stewart the chemist's prescription book shows that he catered as much for animals, particularly horses, as for humans. An entry for 19 October 1918 gives a prescription for Mr. Draffan (miller at Preston Mill), 'to be applied to the horse's fetlocks, night and morning'. Another, dated 29 November 1918, for Mr. Bone of Markle was 'to be applied to the horse's legs'. Mr. Stewart's poison cabinet contained arsenic, strychnine, belladonna and ipecacuanha to be prescribed for all manner of ailments.

Alongside the chemist were boot and shoe makers, tailors, butchers, bakers, grocers, vets, masons, plumbers, joiners, slaters, painters, innkeepers, doctors, bankers, dairymen and motor engineers. An official guide to East Linton, written by Provost Andrew Walker, after whom Walker Terrace is named, published in 1927, lists the following traders:

Alex. Malcolm - grocer and wine merchant
the oldest established grocery business in East Linton
Charles Davidson - boot and shoe maker
hand sewn work a speciality
Robert Dalgleish - grocer and wine merchant
[his telephone number was no.7!]
Thomas Black - baker and confectioner
[his bakery was at Bridge End]
A. Mason - bootmaker
agent for 'Nil Simile', 'Picotee', etc
J. Smith - blacksmith and cycle agent
splendid selection of high grade cycles
Charles McDonald - family grocer
goods delivered daily by our own van
John H. Hutchison - coal merchant and contractor
[his premises were in Bank Road]
W. Burns & Sons - bread and biscuit bakers
marriage and christening cakes a speciality
R. McArthur & Sons - joiners & timber merchants
[their telephone number was no.30!]
John Y. Torrance - chemist
Jonteel toilet preparations a speciality
Horsburgh's Garages - motor and agricultural engineers
[they had premises at High St, Bank Road and Haddington Road]
W. H. Laing - builder and contractor
jobbing. Estimates given

W. H. Laing's remains East Linton's longest surviving business, extending over four generations. The firm was instrumental in establishing the gasworks, as well as erecting many of the town's fine buildings, including Robert Noble's house at no.2 Preston Road. The firm was also the main contractor for the building of the advanced Pasveer sewage disposal plant on the banks of the Tyne to the east of Preston Mill, the first of its kind built in Scotland. This was opened by Provost Rennie in 1971.

In 1932 Lodge Tyneside No.714 purchased the former U.P. Church in Tyne Close for their new premises; since the first meeting of the Lodge, on 13 August 1885, the members had met in Bro. Smellie's Hall in the Red Raw. Fund-raising efforts for the purchase and building conversion included a garden fête at Whittingehame House, whist drives, dances and a 'Name the Doll' competition.

One particular fund-raising venture has left a lasting legacy - *Havers Frae the Linn Rocks.* William Laing, the builder, and Robert Anderson, a joiner, teamed up, called themselves 'Toot,Toot' and 'Pump, Pump' respectively and edited this humorous broadsheet from their head office at 'The Sluice, Linn Rocks'! The *Havers,* with their pithy and witty verses about the town and its characters, proved highly popular, and publication continued until 1939.

Reminiscences of childhood days in East Linton in the years leading up to the Second World War have recently been recalled by a resident:

"Life was simple. We seldom had to go beyond the village boundaries for our needs. Sweeties were cheap. We used to go once a week to the corner shop to buy twopenny worth...Haircuts were performed by the village barber, known to us as Mr. Darling, who sported a moustache impressively twisted and waxed into a long spike on each side of his face. *[Darling's barber shop was at no.34 High St, where The Bake House is today.]*

The dairy and vegetable shop was at no. 32 High Street. It had its own unique smell which hit you as soon as you entered. It was owned and run by Sam Brown, his wife and their two daughters, one of whom was called Beatrice who always seemed to be dressed in the same voluminous ill-fitting brown knitted pullover. The younger sister was called Myra. Mrs. Brown wore visible lace-up boned corsets to keep her ample bosoms in shapely control. If she bent down to pick things up from the floor she often got stuck. Poor old soul. From under the counter you could sometimes hear the 'twang' of the corset bones as they gave up the unequal struggle. We boys always waited with expectation and were seldom disappointed."

HAVERS FRAE THE LINN ROCKS

Head Office:—The Sluice, Linn Rocks. **AUGUST 1933.** **PRICE ? or More. (Inklusive).**

NOTICE

All communications to be addressed to—
THE JOINT EDITORS,
PUMP PUMP, ESQ. TOOT TOOT, ESQ.

Note.
Only 1000 copies of *Linn Rock Havers* for sale daily. Any Fool wishing an extra copy to send abroad will please lodge complaint in writing to the sub-editor on or before Hansel Monday or Rural Trip.

LETTERS TO THE EDITOR

Letter from the Right Hon. Viscount Traprain, Right Worshipful Master of Lodge Tyneside, 714.

DEAR SIR,

I venture to sound the only serious note in your paper, in appealing to your readers to give Lodge Tyneside of Freemasons their help in this endeavour to raise funds towards the reconstruction of their new Temple.

It is unnecessary for me to offer anything by way of explanations of our aims to Brother Masons and, accordingly, I take this opportunity of appealing especially to those outside the craft.

Lodge Tyneside at present hold their meetings in a building which is in many ways unsuitable for the purpose, being too small and inadequately ventilated. In addition to these objections, their lease will expire in two years, and it is by no means certain that they will be able to renew it.

Accordingly, they have purchased a building, the funds for the purpose having been raised entirely by voluntary subscriptions from their members, and are now appealing for your help to enable them to reconstruct it.

By helping Lodge Tyneside in their aim you will not only be helping to endow in East Linton a branch of one of the most ancient orders of mankind, whose influence for mutual help is of a world-wide character, but will also be creating employment among local tradesmen of East Linton.

I am,
Yours faithfully,
TRAPRAIN.

REPLY

DEAR SIR,

It is not in the staff of *Havers Frae the Linn Rock* to be serious, and already we have received several articles and letters which, on account of the seriousness of the matter there contained, we have refused to publish. On receiving yours, however, we decided to give it space in our *Havers*. We trust that your appeal to Brother Masons and others outwith the craft will bear fruit. We know that many copies of our paper will be sent abroad to be read by old Lintonians whom, we hope, will get a little amusement from it, and turn their thoughts to this wee village beside the Linn.

[We beg you to excuse us, Sir, but we cannot do with the serious stuff, and now are with you in your appeal.—Ed.]

This appeal, sent in by Lord Traprain,
Is really for the folk at hame;
So folk ower oor border or abroad
Micht like tae help us wi' oor load.
The auld U.P. Kirk's a fair disgrace,
It'll take some money tae sort the place;
We ken Linton folk have aye been savers,
So when ye read the *Linn Rock Havers*
Gaun tae yer cash box or aul stockin' fit,
We feel shair o't oorsels ye can spare a wee bit.
So dina forget this wee bit appeal,
Send on the lot frae the tae tae the heel;
Donations big or Donations small,
Will always help to build oor hall—
We'll accept postal orders or, if ye like, cheques,
We wid like tae get mair than his Lordship expects.

DONATIONS TO THE *HAVERS* FUND should be addressed to the Secretary of Lodge Tyneside, 714—
R. D. ANDERSON,
18 Walker Terrace,
East Linton,
Prestonkirk,
SCOTLAND.
who will acknowledge same.

Anderson & Son, Tailors

If you want to be well drest,
Just look in, we'll do the rest.
We'll measure you with utmost care,
Before the cloth is sent upstair.
When you stand or when you sit,
We gaurantee the perfect fit.
Our stock comprises shirts and hats,
Collar studs, and fancy spats;
Fancy soxs, and fancy ties,
Overalls in every size.
It fairly sets the neibors' clashin',
When they see o'or stuff oot at the washin'.

Lodge 'Tyneside 714' of Freemasons

PRESENT A

Grand Carnival

IN THE

MEMORIAL PARK, EAST LINTON

ON

SATURDAY, 5TH AUGUST

2 p.m.—11 p.m.

LATEST AMUSEMENTS AND COMPETITIONS FOR ALL—CHILDREN'S SPORTS AND GREYHOUND RACING—DANCING ON SPECIAL DANCE FLOOR—SALE OF CAKE, CANDY, AND PRODUCE—TEAS ON THE GROUND

Admission 6d (including Tax).——Children 2d

GRAND FANCY DRESS PARADE

Assemble in Memorial Park at 6 p.m. for Judging

Prizes will be Awarded for

BEST TURNOUT MOTOR VEHICLE—BEST DRESSED CYCLE—MOST ORIGINAL COSTUME, MOST COMIC COSTUME

Ladies', Gent.'s, and Children's Sections

GRAND OPEN-AIR CARNIVAL DANCE

At 7.30 p.m.——Dance Ticket 1s

FANCY DRESS PARADE

Competitors will please meet in the Memorial Park at 6 p.m., when the Judging will commence. After judging, an organised parade will proceed through the Village. By kind permission of the East Linton Town Council a collection will be taken in aid of The Building Fund, so please be ready for "Ali Baba and the Forty Thieves." The Committee earnestly hope that there will be a large entry in every section.

SO GET YOUR DRESS READY NOW.

CARNIVAL DANCE

A grand Carnival Dance will be held in the Memorial Park after the Fancy Dress Parade. A Special Dance Floor is being erected for this event, and it is hoped to have flood lighting. Tickets are now on sale for the dance, and it would greatly assist if intending dancers would purchase tickets as early as possible. These tickets, price 1/-, may be had from Messrs W. C. TAYLOR, GEORGE RUTHERFORD, MARK SANDIE, THOMAS WHITE, and R. D. ANDERSON. Competitors at the Fancy Dress Parade are requested to attend the Dance in Fancy Dress.

In the event of unfavourable weather the Dance will be held in the Drill Hall.

SPORTS PROGRAMME

1st RACE AT 2.15 PROMPT.

80 Yards Handicap, Girls under 10 years. 80 Yards Handicap, Boys under 10 years.
100 Yards Handicap, Girls under 15 years. 100 Yards Handicap, Boys under 15 years.
Egg and Spoon Race (Girls), Potato Race (Boys), Victoria Cross Race (Girls).
Greyhound Racing (all local dogs), Boys' High Jump (under 15), 100 Yards Handicap (Youths under 18 years), VETERANS' RACE, over 45 years (Handicap).
Ladies' Race, 3-Legged Race (Boys), Skipping Race (Girls) (provide own rope), Obstacle Race (Boys), Place Kick Competition at 3.30 p.m.

EVENING COMPETITIONS AFTER PARADE.

Barrel Boxing Contest, Treacle Scone Race for Boys, Sheafpitching and Pacing Competitions, Pillow Fight.

COMPETITIONS and SIDE SHOWS

PUTTING COMPETITION, CLOCK GOLF COMPETITION, PITCHING COMPETITION
Organised by the East Linton Putting Club.

COCOANUT SHIE—HOOP-LA—THE DANDY—BUCKET AND BALLS—CHINESE LAUNDRY—TIP ME OUT—THE BALL BOARD—SHOVE PENNY—HOUSE—SHOOTING RANGE—THE MAT SLIDE

The Committee take all reasonable precautions to prevent accidents, but it must be understood by Competitors taking part in all events that they do so at their own risk.

R.D.A., *Secy.*

FOR LADIES ONLY

On August—the 5th—there's a grand produce sale, the prices of course will be a' retail, So we're depending on you for tae fill up oor stall, so please send your stuff tae the Masonic Hall. Noo pit on yer girdle and bake a bit scone, send us a pund or ma'be a stone; or heat up the oven and send us a cake, or send us some candy ye see we're no blate, some honey, some floors, or ma'be some eggs, so fill up oor table it his strong enough legs. Now, listen, great news, we're having a jumble, so a' rake thro' the hoose and send us a bundle.

Contributions to the Produce or Jumble Stall will be gratefully received at the Masonic Hall on morning of Saturday, August 5th, between the hours of 10 a.m. and 12 noon, by the Ladies' Committee. So tie a wee bit string on yer finger.

THE LADIES' COMMITTEE
Mrs TAYLOR, BANK ROAD.
Miss WILSON, BANK ROAD.
Miss HORSBURGH, BRIDGE STREET.
Mrs DALGLEISH, THE SQUARE.
Mrs G. GOVAN, THE SQUARE.
Mrs LAWSON, ORCHARD FIELD.
Mrs JAMES STEELE, WALKER TERRACE.
Mrs R. D. ANDERSON, WALKER TERRACE.
Mrs JOHN RATTRAY, BIEL.
Mrs WHITE, LAUDER PLACE.

In the event of unfavourable weather, the Sale will be held in the Drill Hall.

LOST AND FOUND.

FOUND near Drylaw Terrace, 1 pair of brown shoes. If not claimed within three days will be soled.

LOST, between Bridge Street and The Square, bottom set false teeth; age unknown. Finder will be rewarded on returning same to Mill Wynd before top set fall out.

PROPERTY, ETC., FOR SALE.

JOCK RICH has pleasure in announcing to the general public and others that he has been successfully carrying on business as fireworks manager at the Waterin' Stane, and having reached the speed limit wishes to dispose of his fleet of Automobiles (owner pushed) comprising four good wheels (back wheels re-pushed), Bodyguard, painted green (tree colour), Horn in excellent order, Head lamp 40 horse candle power, Tail Lamp lost, fitted with aerial for wireless. Rattlin' car. Fine Xmas Present. Would amuse children and adults. R.S.V.P. *Foreign Papers please Copy.*

R. Dalgleish, The Square

The Editor, Lord bless his face.
Has granted me sufficient space,
In spite o' pressin' local news
To let me here express my views.
Ye ken my shop is in the Square,
My Motor Vans go here and there;
My stock is large comprising hams,
Sauces, pickles, pots o' jam,
Sugar, butter, salt and cheese,
Papers tae for catchin' fleas;
Soap in packets, tins or bars,
And fine selection o' jeely jars.
Paraffin oil, candles and pens
Treacle and syrup, whisky and teas;
Cakes and nice wee rhubarb tarties,
Rice supplied for wedding parties;
Pepper, lemonade and beer,
And lots o' things no' mentioned here;
Eggs, just fresh out o' the nest,
Your order please, I do the rest.

Laing, Builder and Dyker

Ony job requirin' brains,
Sic as cleanin' chockit drains;
Pointin' wa's and sic repairs,
Layin' cement—ashfelt in flairs.
Ye'll find that he is hard tae bate,
For buildin' in an open grate.
Or kitchen range wi' fancy tile,
That fairly makes the water bile.
And when the winter storms dae fa',
He has a squad for shovellin' snaw.
Crazy pavement for your walk,
Laid that ticht there's no a crack.
For miles aroond the Jubilee Tree,
Accounts are rendered a' post free.

Alex. Watt, Housefurnisher

Noo come in folks and gie's a ca',
An' see a shop that's really braw;
Chairs and tables in a raw
For your inspection.
Carpet tacks and spoons and forks
Sic' a collection.
I'm aye at work, I never play,
Oft busy at the turnin' lay,
I'll turn a stick without delay
Without a fault.
And if ye stop inside the day
I'll turn a sommer-sault.

George Laing

[49] The cover of the first Havers.

Jim Menzies

[50] Menzies' Band at a Grand Carnival in the 1930s.
Charlie Kerr (drums), George Pirie (banjo), Willie Nicol (saxophone), Jimmy Menzies (violin) and Jimmy Campbell (accordion). The driver is Jock Gilmour.

At war once more

World War II made its presence felt early in the parish when in October 1939 a German bomber, returning from an air-raid on the Forth Bridge, strafed the area around Preston Mains. In July 1940 another bomber, a Heinkel, dropped two parachute mines at the east end of Traprain Law, one of which exploded creating a deep crater and shaking East Linton. In October 1940 a stick of five bombs was aimed at the by-pass road bridge; one went through the bridge and the others fell into the river, but none exploded. In the following month four more bombs fell on the parish, two in Traprain Field and two in the grounds of Prestonkirk House causing some damage.

After Dunkirk the threat of invasion became very real and defences were constructed along the coastline, at important road junctions and river crossings. The beaches of East Lothian were considered particularly at risk for landings; trenches were dug, concrete tank obstacles erected and poles embedded in the sand to obstruct enemy planes or gliders landing. The Local Defence Volunteers (soon to be renamed the Home Guard) were formed, manned by farmers, those in reserved occupations and those too young or too old to be called up. The weapons were at first primitive, but later some units were organised to perform a secret role from underground hideouts in the event of an enemy landing. There were two of these in the parish, one at Janefield and the other near the entrance to Smeaton.

In 1942 the East Linton Local Defence Committee, chaired by Provost A. P. McCall (after whom McCall Gardens is named), was formed to deal with all local matters related to the war and to work in conjunction with the Home Guard. Among the signals of enemy landings was to be the ringing of church bells (which otherwise remained silent) in the event of parachutists landing, but only if six or more were seen. This precise instruction followed an incident elsewhere in the country when a unit put 'friendly fire' on five of our own parachutists.

As the war progressed, the county's airfields were increasingly used for training aircrews. Tragically, two RAF fighters crashed in the parish; one, a Boulton Paul Defiant from East Fortune, came down behind Drylaw Terrace in poor weather, killing both pilot and gunner, and the other, a Typhoon from 197 squadron based at Drem, crashed in Kingsburgh Gardens killing the pilot and John McDonald, a local man.

Exercises on the coast in preparation for landings in Norway and France resulted in an exclusion zone to the north of Preston Road for anyone not carrying a special identity card. The remains of slit-trenches and rusting corrugated iron can still be seen along the coast above Ravensheugh Sands beside the concrete anti-tank blocks and pill-boxes built earlier in the war to help fend off an invasion.

The reduction in the number of farm workers as a result of young people enlisting presented a serious problem, made even more acute because of the need to bring more land under cultivation. This was partly offset by the Women's Land Army replacing men on the farms and in the market-gardens, and later by German and Italian prisoners.

When the war was over, life for the inhabitants of East Linton and the parish of Prestonkirk returned to normal. However, a critical situation soon became apparent. The Land Girls and prisoners of war, on whom the farmers had depended for manual work, were no longer available, and it was not feasible to return to the number of farm workers of the pre-war years. Yet the heavy tasks of lifting and draining still had to be done. The problem was resolved by the development of hydraulically-operated agricultural machinery, notably the fork-lift attached to the tractor.

East Linton Gala

An old East Linton tradition was revived after World War II. The great event in the East Linton calendar in the first half of the nineteenth century had been the Carters' Play Day (see Chapter 6) but that had ceased about 1865. In August 1934 a 'Grand Carnival' had been held, organised by Lodge Tyneside 714 to raise money for renovating their new premises. During this parade, the Carters' flag was displayed and a burlesque 'crowning' of the 'Linton Lad' and 'Linton Lass' - Messrs. George Wight and Fred Yeats, suitably attired - was carried out by 'Toot, Toot' Laing at the Fountain. A variety of sports then followed in the Memorial Park, and in the evening a fancy dress parade and an *al fresco* whist drive preceded dancing by floodlight to music supplied by Menzies' band. The Carnivals were continued yearly thereafter until the outbreak of war brought them to a close. At the 1939 Carnival, Marion Draffan, the Dux of the Public School, was crowned 'School Queen'.

In 1948 the Royal British Legion revived the idea and the following year held the first 'Gala Day'. Jenny Pringle was crowned the second 'Queen'. In 1963, with the disbanding of the Legion Men's Section, responsibility for running the Gala was taken up by the East Linton and District Community Association, assisted by the local Traders' Association. In 1973, the East Linton Children's Gala Day Association, which had been established the previous year, took over the running of the Gala. Under their first president, Billy Hepburn, they expanded the celebrations once again to cover a whole week of activities, beginning of course with the popular 'Cavalcade on Wheels'. Marion Draffan (by now Mrs. Melville) returned in 1973 to crown her successor, Queen Lynn Kerr, 26th in the 'royal line'. To this day, this band of volunteers, now called the East Linton Gala Association and with long-time president Bill Brodie at the helm, have continued to run the event.

John W. Steele

[51] The coronation of the first Gala Queen, Marion Draffan, in the Memorial Park in 1939.

Modern times

Since the end of World War II, East Linton and the parish of Prestonkirk has seen accelerating change. Many of the old trades and businesses have disappeared from the town, and the countryside around has changed as the result of agricultural improvements.

Most of the farms are now large and arable, intensively cultivated to produce mainly grain crops, mostly barley and wheat. In recent times oilseed rape has replaced sugar beet. Potatoes and vegetables are also important crops. Major developments have been made by plant breeders which has led to an increase in grain yields of 80% per acre. Dairy herds have decreased in recent years and while there are some beef herds, the largest numbers of livestock are pigs and poultry, with sheep on the higher ground.

Meanwhile, in the town the balance has moved away from businesses to residences. Among the greatest losses to the community was the closure in the 1960s of Dod Durie's smiddy; this was adjacent to the plot now occupied by the Memorial to John P. Mackintosh, M.P., at the junction of High Street and Preston Road. Dod, besides being a first-class tradesman, was a great wit, and his premises became the focal point for many retired men who habitually congregated there for a chat and to discuss world affairs.

Perhaps the most momentous change in modern times happened in May 1975 when the Burgh of East Linton was formally abolished and responsibility passed to East Lothian District Council. The act brought to a close more than a century of government by 'the Linton toon council'.

But despite all the changes down the millennia, farming remains the life-force of the town and parish, just as it was 6000 years ago.

John W. Steele

[52] Outside David Durie's smiddy c. 1900.
The photograph, taken by Dod Durie, David's son, pictures David Durie, G. Blackhall and a fish wife, and has been printed from one of Dod's glass plates.

East Linton Town Council

[53] The Town Council's logo, designed by Robert Noble.

On 15 May 1975, the Burgh of East Linton was formally abolished after 112 years of existence. The death-knell had been sounded in 1973 with the passing of the Local Government (Scotland) Act, which vested responsibility for the town's affairs in the newly-created East Lothian District Council.

The Burgh had been created in 1863 as part of a nationwide restructuring of local government and policing. In 1892 the Burgh Police Act further strengthened the town council's powers. For most of its existence, the council met in Smellie's Hall, in the Red Raw in Bridge Street. However, on 24 January 1956 new premises (the present Council Chamber) were opened in the High Street.

We're the Linton toon council - noo aren't we braw,
Jist frae heidquarters up at the Red Raw,
If yer wantin' a sang - it's nae bother at a
Tae the lads o' the Linton toon council.
(R. D. 'Pump,Pump' Anderson, from *A Linton Gathering*, 1967)

Chief Magistrates & Provosts of the Burgh

John Porteous Chief Magistrate 1863-1866
F. Storie Chief Magistrate 1866-1872
John Storie Chief Magistrate 1872-1890
J. Sandie Interim Chief Magistrate 1890
George Smellie Chief Magistrate and later Provost 1890-1893
John Storie Provost 1893-1898
James Watt Provost 1898-1902
Charles Hally Provost 1902-1903
Thomas Muir Interim Provost 1903
William Barrie Provost 1903-1916
Andrew Walker Provost 1916-1934
A. P. McCall Provost 1934-1953
Robert Dalgleish Provost 1953-1956
Miss M. E. N. Aitchison Provost 1956-1965
David M. Rennie Provost 1965-1975

Town Council and Officials at the termination of the Town Council on 15 May 1975

Provost D. M. Rennie
Senior Bailie J. H. Kerr
Junior Bailie J. A. Ogilvie
Hon.Treasurer Miss E. Sandie
Dean of Guild J. Reid
Councillors D. MacDermid
A. Greenan
T. D. Stewart
G. M. Rutherford
Town Clerk J. D. Barlas
Burgh Chamberlain D. Wilson
Burgh Surveyor J. S. Gibson, MBE

John W. Steele

[54] The Territorials march in procession on the day of the United Memorial Service, 20 May 1910, that brought together the congregations of the United Presbyterian Church and St. Andrew's Free Church.

APPENDIX 1

MINISTERS
OF THE PARISH OF PRESTONKIRK

Ministers in Preston Kirk

c.1127 Blahan
c.1188 William
c.1296 Richard
c.1324 Thomas de Gordon
c.1424 Alexander Cairns
c.1463 Patrick Hepburn
c.1494-1503 Gavin Douglas
1503-? John Irland
c.1543 Nicol Crichton
1548-1583 George Hepburn
1586-1596 Robert Hepburn
1597-1618 Edward Hepburn
1619-1669 John Dalzell
1670-1671 John Darngavel (deprived)
1671-1689 George Shiels (deprived)
[1679-1680 Gilbert Rule (deprived)]
1689-1691 John Harvie
1692-1702 John Forrest
1702-1732 Thomas Findlay
1734-1768 Matthew Reid
1768-1808 Daniel McQueen
1809-1841 James Thomson
1841-1843 John Thomson (walked out)
1843-1876 James Porteous
1876-1918 Thomas S. Marjoribanks
1918-1955 Richard Clayton Corrie
1957-1960 Robert Maule Brown
1960-1974 John G. Levack
1974-1986 Kenneth G. Hughes
1986-1998 James B. Lawson
1998- vacant

Ministers in the United Presbyterian Church

1795-1827 Hugh Jamieson
1827-1863 George Paterson
1863-1890 John Park Alexander
1890-1910 Alexander Watt

Ministers in St. Andrew's Free Church

1843-1889 John Thomson
(senior minister from 1876)
1876-1884 Thomas Adamson
1885-1910 Robert G. Rodger

Ministers in the United Free Church

1910-1920 Duncan Blair
1920-1946 John Henderson Edgar
1946-1959 Robert Riddock Fisher

APPENDIX 2

ROLL OF HONOUR
FOR THE TWO WORLD WARS

1914-1918

Adam Johnston
Alex C. Greig
Alex Lawrence
Alex Lockhart
Alex Pennycook
Alex K. Walker
George Greirson
George Laing
George White
Gideon Watt
James Beveridge
James Campbell
James Docherty
James Fraser
James C. Sandie
James A. Tait
James Walker
J. C. Blackhall
John Craig
John Fraser
John Hume
John Logan
John C. McPhail
John Reid
John Storie
John A. Tait
John Wilson
Kenneth Mills
Robert G. E. Stewart
Thomas Aitken
Thomas Greig
Thomas Murdoch
William Aitken
William Currie
William Hood
William S. Logan
William Thomson
William H. White

1939-1945

Alexander W. Manson
David A. Polson
Duncan B. Stewart
George A. McLennan
George M. Munro
John H. Logan
Kenneth L. McLennan
Peter Macfarlane
Robert Taylor
Robert S. Faichen
Taylor Scambler
Thomas W. Briggs
Thomas A. Brown
William Craig

The memorial, an obelisk sculpted from Locharbriggs red sandstone by Alex. Malcolm, of Malcolm & Laing, was unveiled by the Rt. Hon. A. J. Balfour on Saturday 11 September 1920.

APPENDIX 3

EAST LINTON GALA QUEENS

1939	Marion Draffan
1949	Jenny Pringle
1950	Yvonne Hume
1951	Anne Hepburn
1952	Myrtle Chisholm
1953	Jacqueline Malcolm
1954	Liga Viesbarts
1955	Barbara Fowlie
1956	Sheila Glasgow
1957	Mona Virtue
1958	Irene Anderson
1959	Linda McLeish
1960	Ann Scott
1961	Aileen Eadie
1962	Gail Hall
1963	Catherine Fairgrieve
1964	Meta Oliver
1965	Sonia Kordiak
1966	Dorothy Macfarlane
1967	Gail Robertson
1968	Mary Kordiak
1969	Catherine Orde
1970	Lesley Craik
1971	Nancy Butler
1972	Rhona Kay
1973	Lynn Kerr
1974	Glenda Riddell
1975	Pauline Pirie
1976	Marianne Bryce
1977	Lesley Waugh
1978	Diane Curran
1979	Lynn Kennedy
1980	Sally Hunter
1981	Susan Jeffrey
1982	Laurenne Stevenson
1983	Julie Sandilands
1984	Yvonne Logan
1985	Michelle Spence
1986	Laura Simpson
1987	Tracey Spence
1988	Janice Tabraham
1989	Angela Hunter
1990	Louise Scott
1991	Victoria Blackburn
1992	Rebecca Hawthorn
1993	Amy Hoban
1994	Lindsay Orde
1995	Gillian McLauchlan
1996	Rachel Ruxton
1997	Kirsten Wilson
1998	Katy McDougall
1999	Nicola Finnie

LIST OF SUBSCRIBERS

Mary & John Addies
David & Audrey Affleck
George Aitken
G. F. Alderson
Robert Anderson
J. A. Armstrong
Tim Bairston & Joan Simpson
Martin & Katharine Bates
Wilma & Dickie Bathgate
A. P. Begg
Michael & Mauville Beilby
Mr & Mrs G. J. Bell
Mr & Mrs J. T. Bell
W. L. D. Black
Jean Bowie
Harry Boyle
Mrs A. B. Brown
Miss Jenny Brown
Mrs Monica Cameron
Bill & Liz Campbell
Mrs Conchita Campbell
Emma J. Campbell
James & Heather Campbell
Christopher Carter
Jim & Isabel Cheyne
Mr & Mrs Linus Clark
Michael & Aileen Clark
A. F. Clement
Hilary Cochran
Brian & Sandy Coppins
Allison Cosgrove
Barry Craighead
Ian Craik
John Craik
Robert Crail
The Rt. Hon Lord & Lady Cullen
Nancy & Jim Cunningham
Peter & Jean Curran
Ralph Curry & Patricia Steven
Mr & Mrs T. Davidson
David Y. Denholm
Susan & Robin Dickson
Ann & David Dimmock
Mr & Mrs Richard M. Doake
Bill Doig
Greta & David Doig
Pauline Doig
Earle M. S. Douglas
Mrs Audrey Dowling
Ken & Pam Downham
Mr G. Downie
Elizabeth Drever
Roger & Penny Durman
East Linton Primary School
S. Faulks
Ian Fender
David & Fiona Finch
Nicola Findlay
Bill & Jayne Fisher
N. R. Fisher
Jean H. Flockhart
Mrs J. W. Fowler
Elizabeth C. Fraser
James Fraser & Family
John Fraser
Mrs K. M. Gardner
Dennis Garvie
Alexander Gibson
Shirley Gilmour
Margaret & Dave Glass
John F. Govan
Arthur Greenan
David M. Gregory
Ian M. Greig
Stephen Gundry
John G. Guy
Mr & Mrs I. D. Haig
Mrs Anne Hall
Alex & Vanessa Hawthorn
Mrs H. Kay Henderson
Maureen & Bill Hewgill
Mrs L. Hillen
Robin R. Holder
Malcolm Hutchison
Mr & Mrs C. W. E. Jaques
Mrs E. F. Jeffrey
Alison Johnston
George F. Johnston
Dawn Kemp
George Laing
Jenefer Laing
Susan Laing
Marion F. Laing
Mrs Moira Lamont
D. B. Law
Miss Rosemary Leask
Mrs B. Leslie
Ken & Sheila Lochhead
A. T. Logan
Mrs L. E. Logan
Miss Helen Lothian
Mrs Lindy Lynn
James S. Macfarlane
Mrs E. J. Macgregor

TO THE FIRST EDITION

H. Mackay
Mr & Mrs Mackay
Keith & Lorna Maclennan
Mr & Mrs R. Makin
M. A. Malcolm
Lesley Mason
Mary McCall
Marie T. McClure
John McDougall
Mrs Margaret S. McIlhinney
Iain A. & Kirstine McKenzie
Martin & Danusha Melvin
Alan R. Menzies
Garry S. Menzies
J. Roy Menzies
Jim & Jan Menzies
Margaret D. Middlemass
Tom & Marion Middlemass
James Morrison
Miss Murdie
Mr & Mrs T. Murdie
John S. Noble
Mr F. Oakley
William Oldershaw
R. A. & A. M. Oliver
Jim Orde
Les Orde
Linda Orde
Mr & Mrs Norman Orde
Tom & June Ormston
Mrs Elspeth M. Paget
Bill & Shirley Patterson
Mrs C. Paxton
Amanda Pearson
Gael Pollitt
Laraine Pollitt
Adèle Pollitt
Wesley Pollitt
Mr & Mrs F. G. Priest
Dr & Mrs B. Purdue
Hugo & Bryony Purdue
Mick Rae
John & Ellen Reid
Mrs Anne Rennie
Mrs Christine Richardson
Catherine Riley
David & Astrid Ritchie
Elizabeth H. Robertson
J. M. Robertson
Nigel & Frances Ross
Mrs Mary E. Rutherford
Jean Samuel
Mrs Lorraine Scott
Eileen Shaw
Sheena & Tommy Sives
Mrs Vivien Skinner
Mrs Lillian Slarks
Mrs B. Smeaton
Mr & Mrs Bruce Smith
Mr & Mrs A. J. Steele
Mr & Mrs J. W. Steele
Isobel Stephenson
N. G. Steven
Calum Stewart
Mrs Clara Stewart
Jane & Johnny Stewart
K. J. Stewart
Robert & Gloria Stewart
Ian & Sheelagh Stone-Wigg
Miss Elspet A. G. Strang
Miss Romaine Strang
Miss Nan Sutherland
Chris Tabraham
Mrs A. Thomson
Robert H. Thomson
Mrs M. N. Tonkin
Mrs Valerie Travers
Lorraine Turner
Mr & Mrs Turner
D. R. D. Vass
Mary Virtue
Andrew Ronald Walker
A. J. Wallace
John Wallace
Gillian E. Wallace
Mr Leslie Walton
Mr & Mrs P. Wareham
Miss M. L. Warren
Donald Watson
A. Gideon Watt
Jim White & Family
Peg White
Alex Williamson
Jan Winch
Neil Yeats
Brian & Linda Young

INDEX

Further Reading
Sir John Sinclair (ed.) *The Statistical Account of Scotland*, vol. II (1794), pp. 559-64
The New Statistical Account of Scotland, vol.II (1845), pp. 18-28
John Martine *Reminiscences and Notices of 14 parishes of the County of Haddington* (1890), pp. 190-212
Catherine P. Snodgrass (ed.) *The Third Statistical Account of Scotland* (1953), pp. 373-85
Ian & Kathleen Whyte *Discovering East Lothian* (1988)